Your Life Is My INSPIRATION

Your Life Is My INSPIRATION

MY MOTHER'S MEMOIRS

TINA KANE

TRANSLATED FROM RUSSIAN

iUniverse, Inc.
Bloomington

Your life is my inspiration
My mother's memoirs

iUniverse books may be ordered through booksellers or by contacting:

iUniverse
1663 Liberty Drive
Bloomington, IN 47403
www.iuniverse.com
1-800-Authors (1-800-288-4677)

ISBN: 978-1-4759-3116-7 (sc)
ISBN: 978-1-4759-3117-4 (e)

Printed in the United States of America

iUniverse rev. date: 10/31/2012

To all of my wonderful grandchildren.
I hope that as you grow up, you will have a desire to know about your family heritage. This knowledge will spiritually enrich your lives.

With all my love,
Tina Kane
2012

"To be ignorant to what occurred before you were born is to remain a child."

Expression carved on the wall in the Vancouver Library.

CONTENTS

ACKNOWLEDGMENTS

I am grateful to my mother, Sarah Vaysberg, for the precious gift of her life's story. At the age of 80 years old, she was able to capture memories from her childhood through the most crucial periods and events of her life.

This project took me long time to bring to fruition. Many people were helping me along the way. My heartfelt thanks go to my husband, Alexander, for his tireless work on restoring old pictures, which survived World War II and Trans-Atlantic crossing. He respected my mother and treasures her memory.

I am grateful to my son, Stan, for contributing his time and talent. He helped me to express some thoughts in concise language and gave me valuable suggestions.

I am blessed to have friends who were willing to proofread the manuscript and shared their thoughts about the story. Thank you Ellen Kay and Anne Kramer.

Linda Seligson and Esfir Kaganovsky read the manuscript. Their positive feedback encouraged me to proceed with this project.

Last, but not least, my gratitude goes to Linda Love, for applying the finishing touch on the manuscript as well as her genuine support and dedication for bringing this book to life.

Tina Kane, 2012

INTRODUCTION

Immigrants and *immigration* are two words that define America. This country is a magnet that attracts people from all walks of life. In an interview, prior to his first official visit to the United States as French President, Nicolas Sarkozy was asked: "What do you like most about America?" His reply was: "I like about America that this is the only country in the world where a person with the name like Arnold Schwarzenegger can become Governor of the state like California." Opportunities exist for all and that's what is so magic about this country.

In the former USSR, these words were never spoken in a casual conversation among the general population or mentioned in any media such as radio, television, newspapers or books. Nobody, to the best of my knowledge, immigrated to the Soviet Union and those who wanted to emigrate from the Soviet Union were perceived as traitors and therefore enemies of the Soviet State.

My family left the USSR on October 13, 1979. We were among a group of people who were fortunate enough to get exit visas before the start of the war with Afghanistan in December of 1979 and the Moscow Summer Olympics of 1980.

At that time our family consisted of five people: my mother, father, our four-year-old son, my husband and I. The decision to immigrate was two years in the making. My husband and I spent many sleepless nights thinking about our family's future. One of the concerns was the fate of my parents. My husband's mother passed away before we were married. Father remarried and his new wife did not want to leave the USSR.

I was an only child. My parents were both retired and in their sixties when we applied for permission to emigrate from the USSR. They decided to leave behind their friends, sisters, brothers, the place where they had lived for many years, and all the material possessions accumulated over a lifetime and joined my family.

My husband and I were forced to resign our jobs as soon as our employers learned about our intent to emigrate. I was called a "prostitute" at the place of my employment and told by the Personnel Manager that I would die on the streets of New York City from hunger and disease.

Our parents supported us morally and financially during this difficult period in our lives.

Immigration to a country with a different social system, language, culture and customs is never easy. Considering that my parents were *of age,* it was a heroic decision on their part for which I will always be in debt to them. Their only desire was to be with my family.

We waited for over six months for the authority's decision on our applications. After permission was granted, we were asked to leave the country within thirty days. Soon we were stripped of our citizenship. My parents' Social Security payments were stopped immediately upon leaving the USSR.

Each adult member of our family received an "International Exit Visa" as an official document for travel abroad in lieu of a passport. Each person was entitled to exchange one hundred thirty six rubles for ninety US dollars at the State Bank, before leaving the USSR.

The day our family was scheduled to exchange rubles, the State Bank ran out of US dollars. Instead we were given German marks with the majority of money in one-mark coins. When we arrived at our first destination in Vienna, Austria we went to the bank to exchange the German marks into Austrian shillings. We needed money to buy food. The bank teller refused to exchange coins. We were told that only paper money of certain denominations could be exchanged at the bank. This was our first harsh lesson of immigration.

Our next destination was Castel Gandolfo, Italy. We stayed there for two weeks and then moved to a coastal town of Ladispoli. From there we took a bus to Rome and went to the American Embassy. We stood in line for about two hours before entering the building to apply for permission to immigrate to the USA. After a one month wait, the permission was granted.

We arrived in New York City on December 12, 1979. The next day, we flew to Pittsburgh, PA. My mother was in touch with a former colleague who immigrated to the USA two years earlier. She arranged our support through the Pittsburgh Jewish Family Service.

In Pittsburgh it was the first time in my life I saw a public sign "HAPPY HANNUKAH" and a menorah when I walked into the bank on Murray Avenue in Squirrel Hill. I could not believe my eyes and the fact that this Jewish holiday was openly celebrated in America.

With help from the Jewish Family Service we slowly got on our feet. On March 1, 1980, less than three months after our arrival in the USA, my husband began his first job in one of the engineering firms in Pittsburgh.

My parents were a great support to us. They helped us take care of our then five-year-old son, Stan. That allowed me to work and study. We had celebrated Stan's fifth birthday in Italy.

I was accepted to the Carnegie Mellon University graduate program in the Department of Metallurgy and Materials Science. I had earned my undergraduate degree from Kiev Polytechnic Institute. Technical publications, which I co-authored in the USSR and were translated and published in the USA, served as my references. I found them in the Pittsburgh Carnegie Library.

At Carnegie Mellon University, in addition to my studies, I was working as a research assistant on the project sponsored by the National Science Foundation, and was a graduate teaching assistant to one of the professors in our department. That paid my way through graduate school.

During the day, my parents studied English language at the Pittsburgh Jewish Community Center. In the evening, they studied at the University of Pittsburgh. They wanted to be independent from us in their day-to-day lives and looked forward to become US citizens.

Now that I am much older, I can truly understand how difficult it was for my parents to start and adjust to a new life in the USA.

Sadly, my father died four years after our immigration from the USSR. It was Thanksgiving Day, November 29, 1983. He was seventy-two years old. My father's death was a great loss to all of us, especially for my mother. She never complained, but loneliness was hard to hide.

It became even more difficult for her when our family moved from Pittsburgh, PA to Reading, PA in May of 1985. My husband found an engineering position in a local company. By that time we had two children. Our second son, Ariel, was born on March 13, 1984, in Pittsburgh.

The city of Reading did not have an established Russian Jewish Community like Pittsburgh. All of the friends my mother acquired during our five years in Pittsburgh were left behind.

I tried very hard to help my mother overcome the loneliness. I got in touch with the local Agency on Aging. They arranged to pick her up twice a week and take her to the Senior Citizens Center, where she was able to make some friends. She became friendly with a woman, named Francis, who was close to her age, and lived in our development. She also met another Russian woman, Mariya, and became friends with her and her family.

One day I asked my mother if she would be willing to write a memoir about her life. My mother liked this idea. She lived through the extraordinary times of changes in the history of the former Soviet Union. She was the last surviving sibling from a family of ten children. She loved her extended family and had been very close with her sisters and brother, nieces and nephews, staying in contact through correspondence after we emigrated.

Writing a memoir occupied my mother's time and mind, allowing to relive her life over again. I think it made her happy that I was interested in her life's story.

My mother endured many hardships in her life. She faced them with the resolve to better herself and to help others.

Your Life Is My Inspiration

Her life is an inspiration to me. This work is a tribute to my mother's life and an expression of my deepest love and respect for her.

PROLOGUE

My name is Sarah Vaysberg. For twelve years now I have lived
in America, far away from my home, close friends, relatives,
and my favorite job. I left behind everything.

There was plenty of bitterness in the life that I left behind,
but also many unforgettable moments of happiness and joy.
On December 12, 1979, at the age of sixty-eight years old, I
and my husband Alexander Vaysberg, came to America with
our only daughter, her husband and their five-year-old son,
Stan.

We left Kiev, capital of the Ukraine, in search of religious
freedom and with a hope for a better life. On November 29,
1983, I lost my husband. We had been married for thirty-six
years.

On March 13, 1984, my daughter gave birth to a second
child, son Ariel. I helped her to take care of him, so that she
would be able to work.

After seven years of tireless work in America my daughter
and her husband bought a house, where we all currently live.
The house is in a suburb of the city of Reading, Pennsylvania.
There is no public transportation in this part of the city.
Mostly young families live in this development. Almost

everyone works and there are no Russians, or even Americans of my age.

My older grandson is a junior in high school, and my younger grandson is a first grade student in elementary school.

I am home alone the entire day. I am completely cut off from communication with people of my age. I do not drive and that leaves me dependent on others to do it for me. I am lonely. I spend most of my time reading, playing solitaire, taking long walks, and watching television.

My daughter and her husband both work in the same company, which is about 55 miles away from home. They leave early in the morning at 6:00 a.m. and return home at 5:00 p.m., sometimes later. They are always busy taking care of the family, house, daily errands, or problems that may arise.

On weekends they try to entertain me as much as they can. They take me to play bingo, or to see a movie, or to the mall, and occasionally something completely new.

By nature I am an optimist and despite the fact that I am eighty years old, I have retained vivid interest towards life in all its variety. I am the sole survivor among my siblings.

What you are reading now is the result of my daughter's asking me to describe the life of my large family and myself, so that her children will learn about their family roots.

I hope that my story will help you to better understand the meaning of life through the retelling of historic events, which took place during my lifetime, and how they shaped myself as a person and affected the way we lived.

MY FAMILY

I was born into a large family on August 20, 1911, in the village of Nikolskaya Slobodka, behind the pale of settlement. Our village was not far away from the city of Kiev, Ukraine. There were ten children in our family, five boys: Tsezar, Abraham, Levi, Lazar, Michael and five girls: Roza, Etya, Tsipa, Tsilya and myself. I was the ninth child of Pinchus and Shifra Rozin. All children were born healthy, only my youngest brother Michael was born with Down syndrome.

My parents were poorly educated, but hardworking and very religious. They raised us to love each other, to be honest and to help each other. My father was a carpenter and my mother was a homemaker.

Father often left the house to work for wealthy people. They hired him to do different jobs. Sometimes he worked not just as carpenter, but also built small structures such as storage houses, decks and sheds.

Despite the fact that he was not educated, my father understood blueprints very well, and was able to do various jobs. He often helped my older brothers. Together they built bridges across rivers and worked on many other complex projects.

My father's employers respected him. He was known for high quality work. He was an intelligent man with a great sense of humor and always cheerful.

As our family grew, my parents thought about teaching us skills, which we could use to help our family and later on to support ourselves. At that time nobody in poor Jewish families thought about education, only about acquiring a skill, which would make a person self-reliant.

When my oldest brother Tsezar turned eleven years old, my father sent him to his mother, who lived in the city of Mogilev. There he would be able to study the construction trade and to receive a religious education.

My second brother Abraham was very free-spirited. He got involved with a group of young people. Together they studied Karl Marx's theory of capitalism and Lenin's ideas about revolution.

Our oldest sister Roza was very beautiful and talented. She was self-taught and became a dressmaker. Soon she turned out to be known for her skill and earned a living by sewing dresses for a variety of clients. She was also my mother's main helper.

Our house was all the time full of people, friends and acquaintances of my sisters and brothers. We had fun times together and it was always noisy inside. I liked to laugh loudly for any reason and was bursting with energy. I enjoyed playing with the other children and being their *leader*.

My parents were too busy to pay much attention to my upbringing, but I always obeyed their orders and listened to my elders.

Rozin Family
Top row from left to right: Lazar, Etya, Dora (Tsezar's wife), Hilya
(Lazar's wife), Eva (Levi's wife), Levi, Sarah, Ida (cousin).
Second row from left to right: Roza, Tsezar, Father, Mother, Tevi
(Roza's husband).
First row from left to right: Michael and Abraham (Roza's son).
Picture was taken before WWII

REVOLUTION AND CIVIL WAR

We lived in a village of Nikolskaya Slobodka, when Revolution broke out in Saint Petersburg, Russia, in October of 1917. At the beginning we were barely affected by its events. When the Civil War erupted in 1918, dramatic changes were brought upon our daily lives. They were felt not only in the constant changes of the local power in our village, but also in the severe shortages of all common necessities. Even bread became a rare commodity.

By that time only six of us lived in the house with our parents. Both my older brothers Tsezar and Levi got married. Abraham joined the Red Army, and in 1919 was killed in one of the battles against contra-revolutionaries. My oldest sister Roza got married and moved out with her husband Tevi to the town of Boguslav, about 65 miles away.

My first clear recollection about tragic events, which occurred during this time period in our village, left painful memories that lasted forever. I remember that it was a beautiful sunny day. My mother got up early. She made bread dough from the last flour we had left and put it into the oven. She washed the linens and hung them outside the house on the clotheslines, and then called for me.

I was not yet eight years old. My mother told me that she, my father, my brother Lazar and my sister Tsipa would go to Kiev to buy some food. Etya and Tsilya went to school. I would be left in charge of my six-year-old brother Michael, the house, and I must not forget to take the bread out from the oven, when it was ready.

I was home alone with my brother. The moment I took the bread out from the oven, I heard a noise of someone screaming from outside the house. I quickly went out on the street to see what was going on. My neighbor told me that the General Denikin's soldiers came to our village, they killed and robbed Jews, and that it would be best, if I left the house and go into hiding.

I saw my Jewish neighbors carrying valuables from their houses to the houses of our Christian neighbors. I decided that I had to do the same. The most valuable item in our house was a sewing machine. I asked my Christian neighbor to remove the sewing head from the machine, and to help me carry it to his garden. I was going to hide it in the bushes.

After that I picked up my younger brother and carried him to the village Main Square. There I saw a platoon in military uniforms being welcomed by the village elders with the offerings of bread and salt.

Somebody yelled at me, to leave the Main Square, otherwise I would get in trouble. I grabbed Michael in my arms and ran with him to our Christian neighbor's garden. He hid us in the bushes, until in the evening our parents found us. When my mother saw us alive she cried, kissed and hugged us. She thanked God that he saved us. My father expressed his heartfelt gratitude to our neighbor.

After the events of that day, all Jewish men went into hiding in their Christian neighbors' houses. All Jewish women came with their children to our house. We spent a terrible night together. General Denikin's soldiers were searching for Jews. They wanted to kill all Jewish men.

My father was a man of great courage and honor. He felt it was below his dignity to hide in the basement of someone's house. After one week in hiding, he appealed to his Jewish friends. He asked all of them to come out and go to the Chief Official of the village. He intended to tell him about the threat to their lives, and to plead for protection against General Denikin's soldiers.

Everyone was silent. Then my father decided to go by himself. He came out of hiding and went to the Main Square. At the Main Square he saw an officer on a horse and asked for permission to speak with him. After my father delivered the Jewish people's appeal for protection, the officer replied that the problem must be discussed with his superior in Kiev. As soon as the officer departed, two of the General Denikin's soldiers surrounded my father and started to beat him with their clubs.

Someone ran to our house and told us that my father's life was in danger. All the women and children, who were hiding in our house, ran crying to the square. They begged the soldiers to leave my father alone. For a moment the soldiers were amazed and confused by such a large crowd. We managed to grab my father and get him back into the house.

Briefly, the soldiers stood quiet, but then decided to follow us. At the same time, one of our Christian neighbors walked into his house. The soldiers thought it was my father and followed him. This gave us time to escape. The soldiers were very angry that they let my father get away. They began asking people on the street where our house was.

They managed to find out, walked into our house and began breaking everything. They asked Christian hooligans to help them to destroy our modest possessions. The hooligans took all that they were able to carry. The attacks on the Jewish homes continued for the rest of the day.

After the day had passed, my mother became afraid for the lives of my father and her older children. She insisted that my father, my sixteen-year-old brother Lazar and my sisters Etya, Tsipa and Tsilya immediately leave the village of Nikolskaya Slobodka and head for Kiev. Mother, Michael and I stayed behind. My mother hoped to save some of our belongings, but she was afraid to enter the house. We spent the night in the back yard of one of our Christian neighbors, hiding behind pieces of wood.

In the morning the pogrom began once again. All Jewish houses were raided and my mother decided that it was too dangerous to stay in the village. By sunset we also started to head out towards Kiev to join the rest of the family.

We did not have relatives or friends in Kiev. Our family settled in the hotel, where all the other displaced people from the surrounding villages gathered. Life in the hotel was not only difficult for a large family, but it was also dangerous. Every night there was a search for the Bolsheviks and young men by militia, who held power in the city.

One day, in search of food and work, my father met on the street his former employer, Mr. Koptilov. He told him about our family's sufferings. Mr. Koptilov owned a large apartment building on the Pushkinskaya Street. He lived there with his wife and son. He offered our family to move in and rented us an apartment. My father gladly accepted his offer.

The winter of 1920 was very cold with lots of snow. There was no wood to heat up all the rooms in the apartment, and we all settled in one room with a wood-burning stove. That is how we survived the winter.

In the summer of 1920, my sister Roza came to Kiev with her husband. She settled in one of the rooms in the same apartment.

At the end of our rental lease, Mr. Koptilov called upon my father and told him to look for another apartment. At this time it was much easier to find a new place. Soon my father rented an apartment, not far away from where we lived. When we began packing our belongings, Mr. Koptilov told my sister Roza that he would allow her and her husband to stay. He rented them one of his larger rooms. They stayed in this room until the outbreak of the Great Patriotic War[1] on June 22, 1941.

Our new apartment was on 14 Podvalnaya Street. The building was big and housed many families. There was a large courtyard. We settled in one of the lower level apartments with three rooms.

During the year of 1920 life was very difficult. Food was scarce, bread with butter and salt was considered a treat, and we did not have sugar for our tea. A day when we had hot cereal was considered a holiday. In spite of all the difficulties, we children did not suffer too much. I always had a company of friends, and a great time playing with them in the courtyard. I did not think about what was going on in the outside world.

In the fall of 1920, I was sent to study in a private school, which was located in the same building where we lived. Unfortunately, I did not study for long. In the winter of 1921, typhus started to go around, and people got sick at a rapid pace. Our sister Tsipa became ill.

---

1 World War II on the territory of the Soviet Union.

My mother did not want her to be taken to the hospital, which was already packed with the victims of that dreadful disease. We lived in a separate apartment. Tsipa was allowed to stay home. My mother cared for her. She would not leave her bedside day and night, but none of the efforts helped. After one week Tsipa died.

This event was a great tragedy for all of us, especially for my mother. Tsipa was truly her favorite. We all loved her dearly. She was very tender and hardworking. Somehow she always managed to protect us from anything considered wrong. My mother was completely in a state of shock and depression. She did not talk, and became indifferent to what was going on around her. She did not smile anymore.

As the young child I was left completely without any supervision and guidance. I was forbidden to attend school after my sister got sick. I spent most of the time outside in the courtyard of our apartment building, playing with the other children.

In February of 1921, my sister Roza gave birth to a baby boy. She named him Abraham, in honor of our brother, who perished during the Civil War. When Abraham turned one, she decided to take me to live with them. She needed help to run errands around the apartment and tend to the baby.

In 1922, during the NEP[2], all the other members of our large family who had survived the Civil War, moved to Kiev. My brothers Tsezar and Levi each rented an apartment for their families on the same street where Roza lived.

I often took my one-year-old nephew Abraham to play in the courtyard of the apartment building where my brothers

---

2 New Economic Policy proposed by Vladimir Lenin. Form of a State Capitalism allowing some private ventures in order to spur economic growth.

lived. The courtyard was big, and there were many children to play with. We all had a great time. I lived like that for several years, helping my older sister and brothers with their small children. Nobody thought about me growing up, while not attending school and getting an education.

During that period significant changes occurred in the life of my parents. My father was a very religious man. He always attended Shabbat Services at the synagogue, but none was close enough to where we lived. One day he saw an advertisement for a carpenter position, wanted to renovate an old building into a Jewish House of Worship. The building was situated in the courtyard between two big apartment buildings. It used to be an old mansion, which belonged to a wealthy family. The family fled to France after the Revolution. The house had a large ballroom with a balcony and several other smaller rooms.

My father applied for the position and was hired to renovate the house. After all the repairs had been made, he was offered a job as a custodian, and given two rooms to house his family. We moved to a new place.

Everyone in my family worked or studied, except for me. My sister Etya understood the importance of education. She demanded that my parents take me back home and let me get a basic education. I was almost eleven years old and well behind children of my age in educational level.

My parents agreed and hired private tutors to prepare me for school, but I did not want to study. I greatly enjoyed romantic novels, and could easily stay up all night reading books. Etya showed great perseverance and helped me with my studies. In 1923, I was accepted into the fourth grade of the Labor School No. 6.

SCHOOL YEARS

At the beginning, I did not have any friends in school and felt extremely insecure. Students accepted me with a little bit of hesitation. After eight weeks of study, I became friendly with several girls in our class. Some of them would later become my life-long friends.

Teachers in our school were mostly middle aged and older individuals from the former private schools. Our homeroom teacher was Nina Ivanovna. She was between forty-five and fifty years old and styled her hair like a man. She was a tall woman and wore only low heel shoes. She was always dressed very conservatively. Nina Ivanovna was a great teacher and showed her devotion to each of us. Students trusted her and always turned to her with their personal problems.

During the post-Revolution years, many children were very religious. They regularly attended church, prayed to God, and observed all the religious holidays. In our class, one girl named Katya Kadushkina, was a very eccentric person. She always spoke about God with great passion, and told everyone that they must trust in God.

We turned to Nina Ivanovna for her guidance and explanations. This was a confusing time for all of us. Our teachers taught us that God and religion should not be a part of our lives. We were told that religious freedom was not something Communists wanted to teach a young generation.

Nina Ivanovna taught Social Studies. She tried to explain to us that we must respect people who trust in God. She told us that we live in a period of great changes in our society and that it will take a long time to change people's ideology, beliefs, traditions and customs. She made clear to us that only through education would each person be able to decide for him or herself if God exists.

She invited two religious girls, me and three others to her apartment. When we walked inside, the first thing that we noticed was an icon in the corner of the room. The light was shining down upon it. Nina Ivanovna explained to us that her mother lived with her, and was very religious. She thought it would be wrong to try and change her mother's beliefs, and that religion should be able to be practiced in one's home. We talked about our families and she told us stories of her life. We all had a wonderful time.

My other remarkable teacher was Mr. Tarachovsky. He taught mathematics. He loved his subject and educated us how to find the joy in solving mathematical problems. Some girls even had crushes on him. We had many other wonderful teachers, but these two individuals were the most brilliant and left their mark in my heart.

I was not very well prepared for school and was placed in the fourth grade. With a great desire for learning, I developed an ambition: I wanted to become a better student. I worked very hard and soon turned out to be a very good student. Mathematics became my favorite subject. I befriended many of my classmates. We often had parties and outings after school was over and on the weekends.

My two best friends were Frida Weitzman and Tanya Podolsky. They both had difficult lives. Frida's father had been killed during the Civil War. Her mother was paralyzed from a stroke. She had three sisters and one brother. Frida was the youngest. They all lived in the same apartment and did not have any relatives in Kiev.

We became not just friends, but members of each other's families. Frida grew to be much like a daughter to my parents. She was very beautiful and generous, always ready to share whatever small possession she might have with her friends. Frida was a favorite in her family. Everyone tried to do whatever was possible to please her. This turned out to have a negative consequence during her adulthood. She never accepted compromises in her life.

Tanya Podolsky was an orphan. Her parents perished during a Jewish pogrom. She managed to survive by pure luck. She lived with her mother's sister. Her aunt was very strict and demanded that Tanya follow a certain set of rules. After school, Tanya was not allowed to go out and play outside. She helped her aunt with all the household chores. Not withstanding her strict lifestyle, Tanya was always cheerful, and never complained. We were not allowed to visit Tanya in her aunt's apartment.

In the same apartment building with Tanya lived another girl who went to our school. Her name was Manya Choletsky. Her father was killed during the Civil War. Manya lived with her mother, younger sister and three brothers. Her family liked Tanya very much. They felt sorry for her and always invited Tanya to their apartment, when she was free. I became a very good friend with Manya.

In school we often had homework that required us to memorize poetry. My friends and I kept a diary of our favorite poems. I loved Pushkin, Lermontov, Nekrasov, Esenin and other famous Russian poets, and memorized many of their poems. We often organized literary meetings and attended literary concerts.

My life was interesting. I did not feel the difficulty of the day-to-day struggle to survive. Food was scarce, but all I needed was a piece of bread or bagel. Most important, I was concerned with my education, friends, and the good times we had together.

Life-long friends

Manya Choletsky (left) and Frida Weitzman

Sister Tsilya and brother Lazar 1926

Sister Etya
Year taken unknown

At the same time major changes took place in our family. Seven people lived now in our household. My parents, Lazar who was twenty, Etya who was eighteen, Tsilya who was fourteen, I who was thirteen, and our youngest brother Michael who was eleven.

Lazar went to work as a painter for the Construction Company. Tsilya and I were still attending school. In our family my sister Etya was the first one who truly understood the importance of education. She taught all of us that we must be good students and eager to learn. She preached that in the new Socialist Society the future belongs to the educated.

The main requirement for the college or university admission was to be from the working class or the poorest peasant class family. Etya dreamed to be admitted to a school of higher education. In order to achieve that, everybody was required to have a *stazh*, which at that time meant a work experience as a laborer for at least two years. Etya joined Lazar and accepted a very low paying job with a construction company. This was hard labor, but she refused to give up.

In 1925 the Soviet government began its greatest campaign against religion. Churches, synagogues, prayer houses and other religious institutions were either destroyed or closed down. The government seized the prayer house where my father worked and our family lived. We were forced to move out.

My parents rented a two-room apartment in the raised basement of the nearby building. My family and I lived there until the outbreak of the Great Patriotic War in June of 1941.

My sister Tsilya graduated from the Labor School in 1925, and went to work as an apprentice at a footwear factory. She worked in the sewing department. Etya continued to work during the day and went to school at night in order to complete her secondary education and get a High School Diploma. I graduated from the seventh grade of the Labor School No. 6 in 1927. This was considered the end of the general secondary education.

All schools during that period were Labor Schools. The goal of the educational system was to provide general education for the young generation, and to familiarize students with the basic knowledge and skills, demanded by the growing industries.

One of the ways this was achieved, was through organizing frequent visits to various industrial facilities, where students had an opportunity to be exposed to different technologies. This method was used to help school graduates to have an easier transition from a learning environment to a working environment.

Children of the working class parents were urged to continue towards higher education. The Soviet government wanted to create a *new intelligentsia* from the class of citizens, who were deprived of educational opportunities before the Revolution, and did not want to rely solely on the expertise of the *old intelligentsia* from the former privileged class.

My brother Lazar was accepted to the Structural Engineering Institute in Kiev. He accumulated enough *stazh* hours to be qualified for admission. At the beginning, he had a difficult time with his classes. He was very bright and hardworking. Soon he made many new friends and they all studied together. Etya helped him as much as she could.

My former Labor School had been converted to a Vocational School. The new school offered students, who had completed seven years of the Labor School, a continuation of their secondary education, and provided training in different occupations. Vocational School was equipped with laboratories and shops, to train students in their chosen specialty. My family agreed to enroll me into the Vocational School. I was again surrounded by young people of my age. We were free from the care of supporting ourselves and concentrated on our studies.

The same teachers from the Labor School No. 6 taught general education courses. New teachers taught only specialty vocational courses. Students in my class were friendly, and we often gathered together in each other's apartments for parties, meetings and discussions.

At the same time a variety of new clubs were opened for the workers. These clubs invited different performers and artists to present their work. They served educational, cultural and social functions. We often attended these clubs in our free time.

My old school friends each went their own way through life, after graduation from Labor School No. 6. Frida Weitzman moved to Kharkov and continued her education there. Manya Choletsky was accepted to a Commerce School in Kiev and we often saw each other.

Tanya Podolsky did not continue her education past secondary school. Later on she married a blind man. He was a piano tuner. Tanya learned her husband's unique skill and helped him in his work. They had two beautiful daughters and a very happy marriage. I lost touch with Tanya in later years. Frida and Manya remained my life-long friends. Our friendships endured.

In the Vocational School I met new friends. One of my best friends became Sonya Tabunchikova. She lived with her mother and older sister on Sofievskaya Street. Her mother was a dressmaker.

The Examination Committee was comprised of seven teachers. I walked into the room by myself, and was very uneasy. I was asked questions and was given time to prepare my answers. I answered all the questions, and received good grades on all subjects. I was awarded a High School Diploma. This was an accomplishment in my situation. I was very happy and proud.

During the same period other changes took place in our family. My brother Lazar married Etya's good friend. Her name was Hilya. He moved out from our small apartment to his wife. Etya herself was admitted to a very good engineering school, Kiev Polytechnic Institute, which had long being her dream. My other sister Tsilya also got married and moved out to her husband.

To speed-up recovery, my doctor arranged a trip for me to a health spa in the town of Slavyansk, in the western Ukraine. I was unable to take this trip by myself. I was still walking with the aid of crutches. Etya had one week before the start of the fall semester. She volunteered to be my escort and helped me to get to the health spa, by practically carrying me. The streets in this town were dangerous for me to walk on with the crutches by myself.

I spent one month in the health spa. My improvement from the various treatments was almost negligible. My toes and heel still moved very little, or not at all. I was put on a train with the help from the health spa personnel, and my relatives met me at the railroad station in Kiev.

When I arrived home, I learned that the Department of Metallurgy at the Kiev Polytechnic Institute, which Etya attended, had moved from Kiev to Leningrad[3]. Students, who wished to continue their education, were given an opportunity

---

3 Presently Saint Petersburg.

to be transferred to a school in Leningrad. Etya moved out there to continue her education. Only my parents, my brother Michael and I now lived in our apartment.

I felt depressed at the time, and did not know exactly what to do with myself. I was unable to work and it was too late to apply for college. By that time, every college completed their admission examination trials, and the fall semester had already begun. I stayed in such a gloomy mood for about two weeks.

One day, reading our local newspaper, I learned that a new college would soon be opening in Kiev, College of the Leather Technology. Applications for admission were solicited.

I still was unable to walk freely on my own, and asked my mother to invite my brother Tsezar's wife Dora to our apartment. She was the only one who did not work at the time. I asked Dora to go to the college and find out their admission requirements. She was able to secure an interview with the college President for me.

I prepared all the required documents, wrote my autobiography and with the help of my sister-in-law was able to get to the college for an interview. During an interview, I was told that there was only one vacancy left for a student in the Industrial Engineering Department. The semester had already begun. I asked the college President to review my credentials and to consider me for the vacant spot. After my grades and other required documents had been reviewed, I was accepted.

COLLEGE YEARS

I started college on November 1, 1930. In my class the majority of the student body was comprised from people who held responsible positions in industry, but did not have the proper education to be effective managers.

There were a total of twenty-five students in my group, which encompassed people from different professional backgrounds, ages, and levels of education. Only seven students were close to my age and only six students, including myself were females, the rest were men.

All the females were high school graduates. Among the men, only two had High School Diplomas. The rest completed a special short-term intensive course of study to prepare them for entering college.

Taking into consideration our different educational backgrounds, the college administration insisted on a group study method. The students, who came to college with the stronger academic background, were assigned to help those who needed extra help with their study.

Despite the diversity in my class, students were generally friendly. The college lifestyle, combined with the group study method, helped make us feel closer to each other. Over time the boundary separating us by our ages began to fade. We helped each other not only with our education, but also with personal problems.

Professors and faculty members demanded high academic standards from us, especially in areas dealing with the industrial economics and mathematics. Some of the faculty members combined teaching and work in the industry.

I immediately became part of the group and very friendly with Fay Sepenuck and Sonya Dubinsky. They both lost their parents during the Revolution and Civil War, and as a result lived most of their lives in orphanages. When they were accepted to college, Fay went to live with her older sister and Sonya moved in with her older brother.

During the post-Revolutionary period, thirty to forty percent of the studies consisted of practical training for the industrial jobs. Our first internship was at the leather manufacturing factory not far away from Kiev. During internship we were introduced to every stage of the leather processing and products manufacturing.

In September of 1931, one evening when students gathered together for socializing, local Communist Party Leaders approached our group. They introduced themselves and asked that all the men from the group appear the following morning at the regional chapter of the Communist Party Headquarters.

When our friends left the next morning, we waited for them hour after hour, but nobody showed up. By the end of the day we became very concerned and began to worry about them. They finally came back early in the morning on the next day. Everyone looked grim and worn-out.

They did not want to talk about what had happened, and answered none of our questions. We insisted that they tell us what had happened. At last they broke the silence. We were asked not to mention to anyone what they were about to tell us, because it would put their lives, and the lives of their loved ones in jeopardy.

We were told that the local Communist Leaders had asked our friends to help fight with the *Kulaks*[4], who were hard working peasants. They produced grain, meat, milk, fruits and vegetables and provided food for the cities population by selling their goods at the farmer's markets.

Communists declared them *as enemies* of the Soviet State. Their properties were confiscated, their harvests were taken from them by force, and many heads of the households were arrested and taken to prison. Some, who strongly resisted the Communists' orders, were shot to death on the spot in the presence of their wives and small children. Young children were taken away from parents, and adult members of the families were sent to Labor Camps in Siberia. The picture was gruesome.

We promised never to reveal to anyone, the tragic events that took place before our friends' eyes. What we learned left a horrible fright in our hearts.

The industrial internship was very intensive. Everyone had to work and to learn the process of leather manufacturing from the initial to the final stage. The areas covered from the receiving, where skins from the killed animals were collected, to the shipping floor, from where finished leather was sent to different factories all over the country.

During the years I studied in college, my industrial internships led me to most of the largest leather manufacturing factories in the Ukraine and to "Skorohod"[5], a footwear factory in Leningrad, Russia.

---

4 Kulak means "fist" in Russian Language.
5 Skorohod means "fast walker" in Russian Language.

My first two years in college went by without any major events, until my junior year. I must admit that I was of an ordinary appearance. I was never popular for my looks. Everybody always said that I was a person of great character, and that made me well-liked among my friends. I was popular among students in my group, as well as students from the other departments, especially men. I never took these relationships seriously and only considered them as nothing more than friendship.

Suddenly, I noticed a very special affection towards me from one of my friends. His name was Vladimir Kovalev. He was eight years older then I. Vladimir distinguished himself from the other students with his very neat appearance. He was always dressed tidily and overall very well groomed. Vladimir was of an average height, and had a body build that made him look rather athletic. He had blond hair, beautiful blue eyes and possessed a very pleasant disposition.

Vladimir came to Kiev from a small town named Belaya Tserkov. He received his secondary education at a local technical school. His father had worked most of his life building railroads, and his mother was a homemaker.

Vladimir always tried to talk to me in between classes, and was eager to do any sorts of favors for me, no matter how small. After we had taken finals in our sophomore year, Vladimir asked if he could walk me home. I noticed that he looked pretty nervous, but I said *yes* anyway.

While we were walking, he suddenly turned towards me and said that he was in love with me, and only death could ever make him stop loving me. Vladimir started going on about me, saying that I was the first woman to truly agree with his ideals, that I was extremely charming, had a very warm heart and sincere soul. He told me that I was genially caring for the others, very intelligent and had a remarkable personality.

Vladimir expressed his feelings very emotionally, and this made a lasting impression. I wanted to calm him down, and to take control of the situation. I replied that he had great imagination and idolized me. I was very surprised with his deep feelings towards me, but I did not reciprocate the same towards him.

Vladimir looked very upset, but tried to stay composed. He said that the way I responded was truthful, and it helped to reinforce the image he had of me. He admitted that my reply was like a dagger in his heart, and that he could not stop thinking about me. He affirmed that he would try everything in his power to win my heart over, and that he would never give up.

The entire situation left me feeling a little disturbed. I told Vladimir that we still had two more years of college together, and that perhaps the relationship between us might change in the future. After these words we parted.

Later on I learned that Vladimir had been so crushed by my response, that he left college without completing his finals, and went home to Belaya Tserkov. After vacation he returned to college. He took his examinations during the summer and was able to continue his education.

When fall semester began, Vladimir confessed to me that he had been extremely lonely during vacation. He had spent most of his time at the park overlooking a river, just trying to avoid company. During that time, he had written many poems, and had dedicated them to me. After that, it was difficult to avoid him.

Everybody in our class noticed his feelings towards me. All my friends, who knew about Vladimir and me, for the most part supported him. If any other young man tried to approach me, my friends would do their best to alienate him, by making jokes, unpleasant remarks and so on. This forced another fellow to disappear.

As it turned out, Vladimir was a good athlete. He was particularly fond of ice skating. We often went skating together at the local ice skating ring. I was not a very good skater, but with Vladimir's help and holding his hand, I was not afraid to be on the ice.

I gradually grew to like ice skating very much. Vladimir always packed away my skates and sweater into his backpack, so that I would not have to carry them, which was very nice of him. When I would get my belongings back, my skates were always sharpened and my sweater had a scent of perfume. Vladimir was also a very good swimmer and enjoyed rowing. Sometimes we rented a boat and went for a ride on the Dnieper River.

College friends
Top row: Sarah and Vladimir
Bottom row names unknown

When summer came, and it was time to apply for the internship, Vladimir applied for a position in the same city I did. As fate would have it, we both were accepted. Each of us worked for a different company in the beautiful city of Odessa, a busy port on the Black Sea.

We spent most of our free time together. Vladimir and his friends bought a gramophone. We often had parties where we would enjoy dancing. Vladimir liked to bake and always prepared delicious desserts for our gatherings.

In the fall of 1932, all the students from our college were sent to help harvest crops. As a result of the famine, many peasants had died and there were not enough people to work in the fields. Living and working conditions in the village were appalling. We did not have any equipment to assist us, and all the harvesting was done manually, which proved to be extremely difficult.

In the village people were dying in front of our eyes. Seeing children suffering was especially difficult to bear. For years to come, the consequences of the 1932 famine were felt by all. The people of the Soviet Union were used to the harsh living conditions, shortages of food, clothing, and almost every kind of necessities. Everybody tried their best to cope.

Throughout my college years survival was a way of life. Although times were tough, I always believed that better days will come. Everybody hoped that in the future they would have plenty of food, clothing, comfortable living conditions and everything required for a normal life. Unfortunately, our dreams did not come true. Our entire lives were one big struggle to survive.

In the summer of 1934, my sister Tsilya and her two-year-old son went on vacation to Boguslav. This was a very picturesque town with a quaint river, named Dew. In August she wrote a letter, inviting me to come and spend several weeks with them. During my years in college I had never gone on vacation. I always tried to find work. This was my last summer in college. I decided to join my sister.

She rented a room in a private home with a garden. The owner allowed us to pick fruits and vegetables that had grown in his garden. We spent most of the day on the beach at the Dew River. One day on the beach, I spotted a young man with a nice athletic body. He also noticed us, and came over to say *hello*. He was from Boguslav, and was visiting his parents during the summer. His name was Peter. He had recently completed his compulsory military service in the Red Army, and was a student in the University of Kharkov.

We had a lot of common interests to talk about. He was a very good swimmer, and we went together for a swim. Peter walked us home, and asked if he could join us at the beach the next day. From then until the end of our summer vacation, we spent most of our time together. He was a nice looking man, and had many interesting stories to tell us about his years of military service.

He also showed a great deal of interest in me. My sister liked him a lot, and insisted that I showed my interest in him. I would just reply to her that Peter was simply bored by himself, and was only looking to have company during summer vacation. I never thought highly of myself, and in no way was self-confident.

Two days before we were going to leave for Kiev, he suddenly began talking about how beautiful my eyes were, how good he felt around me, and that he would like to continue seeing me in the future. Peter told me that he had a brother who lived in Kiev, and he would like to visit him before going back to school. On the day of our departure he walked us to the train station.

A few days later he was in Kiev visiting his brother. While there, he spent most of his time with me, and met my family. When Peter left, I began receiving letters from him. Our correspondence did not last long. I stopped responding to him because of my relationship with Vladimir. I did not want to prolong and deepen our involvement. In the future years, life brought us together on two separate occasions. Once we met after my graduation from college, and second time at the end of the Great Patriotic War. Regrettably, circumstances did not favor to continue our relationship, and we went our separate ways in life.

This was my last year in college. I had to prepare for my finals and to complete my pre-diploma internship. After some consideration, I applied for the internship at a footwear factory in Leningrad and so did Vladimir. A total of four students from our college were accepted as interns to this factory: me, Vladimir, my friend Fay, and one of the few married students in our class, Eve.

We all dreamed of visiting Leningrad. We heard about its magnificent beauty and really wanted to experience the culture and history of the city, founded by Peter the Great.

Four of us managed to rent a small apartment. Women lived on one side, and Vladimir stayed in his own designated area. Vladimir was a real gentleman. He got up earlier than we, started the samovar, made us tea, and prepared a modest breakfast for all of us. After breakfast we took a bus to the factory, where each of us worked in a different department.

After work we would always go to see something new and interesting. Every street had its own history and great beauty. On weekends we visited famous museums. We attended

Hermitage, Museum of Russian Art, Isaac Cathedral, Kazan Cathedral and many others.

We went to Petergof to see czar's summer palaces with their beautiful fountains and gardens. We took a tour to Tsarskoye Selo, where famous poet Alexander Pushkin attended school for the children of Russian Nobility. We tried to see as much as possible during our stay in Leningrad. We were greatly impressed by the city's architecture and monuments, gardens and bridges, wide prospects and magnificent squares.

In the evening, we tried to attend theaters, concerts, exhibitions and everything this city with its rich cultural life was able to offer. We usually bought the cheapest theater tickets available. The Mariinsky Ballet and Opera Theater was our favorite. Our lives were much fulfilled.

Vladimir would always surround me with special attention. One particular occasion left me with a very kind impression of him. We bought in advance tickets for a very popular show. On the day of the show, I was not feeling well. Vladimir said that he would not leave me home alone. I told him that he should go, since there was nothing he could do to help me. Tickets were quite expensive for us, despite being the cheapest ones you can buy. It was just a common cold and all I needed was rest. Vladimir refused to go.

When our internship ended, we were all excited and culturally enriched with everything we saw in Leningrad. At the same time we were eager to go back home. Returning to Kiev, would mean that our lives as students were coming to an end, and that each of us would go their own way through life. Everyone was thinking about what they will do after graduation.

Every student in our class had to take several specialty subjects, pass final exams, and present a graduation diploma project. For my graduation diploma, I chose a project dealing with the development of a specialized factory, geared towards making children's footwear. This was a very difficult project. I had to take into account the technological and economical effectiveness of such a factory and substantiate its profitability.

I had to work very hard. At that time, there was no children's footwear factory in the USSR, and no example for me to study. Many professionals from the Ministry of Light Industry expressed genuine interest in my project. I was offered a chance to present my diploma project, not only to a college faculty, but also to the representatives from different industries. They would evaluate my ideas.

Due to tremendous interest in my project, I was asked to present my diploma at the Footwear Factory in Kiev. This was a great honor, and I was very nervous. Only a few students were offered an opportunity to present their diploma project in front of such an important audience. The date I was scheduled to give my presentation was December 2, 1934.

On December 1, 1934, a great tragedy affecting the political life of the entire country occurred. A very prominent political leader, Sergey Kirov, was assassinated in his office in Leningrad. He was highly respected and liked by the public, and everyone was shocked and saddened by the news.

He was considered one of the most prominent political leaders of that time and was seen as a head of opposition to Joseph Stalin's increasing hold on power. Nobody knew who the real assassin was, and nobody could predict the tragic events of the *Great Purge*[6], which would follow.

---

6 Great Purge of 1937-1938. Its goal was to sweep away all of Stalin's "enemies" by execution or lengthy prison terms in Siberian labor camps.

I was profoundly affected by this sad news, but tried to concentrate on my presentation the following day. Members of my large family were not particularly interested in my diploma project presentation. Everybody was busy with their work, family, and day-to-day survival. Only my sister Roza, showed interest in attending my presentation.

As if the news of Kirov's homicide and the lack of support from my family were not big enough distractions, I was also developing a fever, and was not feeling well. I knew that it would be absolutely impossible to reschedule and canceling was out of the question.

Many high ranking individuals from the Ministry of Light Industry, representatives from the industry, and members of the faculty and college administration were going to be in attendance.

Vladimir accompanied me to my presentation. He helped me to set up all the display materials, and tried to ease the stress by telling jokes and cheering me up.

The large room began filling up with people, most of whom I did not know. The Presiding Committee consisted of the college faculty members and administration, representatives from the Ministry of Light Industry and the Director of the Kiev Footwear Factory.

The total time of my presentation with a question and answer session lasted over three hours. I do not remember how I presented all my material or exactly how I answered the questions.

At the conclusion of my presentation everybody congratulated me with a job well done. My sister also said that everything went very well. Her presence provided me with a sense of great support and comfort. I was awarded the highest grade possible on my graduation diploma project. Afterward, I received several excellent job offers.

Following graduation everyone was having a party. My group of friends decided to reserve a section in the restaurant, in one of the best city hotels "Continental." As I already described, those years of study were filled with the hardships, and we lived in poverty. I did not have a nice dress or shoes to go to a party at the restaurant.

My sister Roza happened to have a black silk dress she could give me. The dress was very nice, but a little bit plain and did not fit me that well. As a graduation gift, she altered it to fit me and decorated it with white lace. She turned it into an elegant and beautiful dress. My brother Tsezar and his wife Dora bought me a pair of shoes from the consignment store. This was their graduation gift.

I was never dressed so nicely in my entire life. I looked and felt real good. Roza attended the graduation party with me. She heard a lot of compliments said about my efforts by the college faculty members and from my friends. After the party she told me that she was very proud of what I had accomplished. Later on at a family gathering, Roza told everybody of the work I had managed to do, and how proud they all should be of me.

After graduation, Vladimir accepted a job offer in the city of Artiomovsk. I accepted a position with an Administrative Office in Kiev. This office oversaw all footwear factories in the Ukraine. It was considered a very prestigious offer.

We both knew that the distance between us would be a great difficulty for our relationship. We both were going to try and stay true to one another. I told Vladimir that distance and new surroundings would be a great test of our feelings towards each other. Vladimir replied that he was confident his love for me would endure any distance, and did not require any test.

He said that he did not want to interfere with success in my professional career. Vladimir promised, that after completion of his mandatory job assignment, he will come back and we will be together again. After graduation each of us felt a sort of emptiness. We missed our friendship and our way of life in college.

NEW BEGINNINGS

On January 1, 1935, I began my new job. I went to the Personnel Department where my position title was decided. I was assigned to work as an Industrial Engineer in the Department of Labor, which I accepted.

The Department Manager was a middle aged man. On my first day he introduced me to everybody in the department and described my duties. My assignment was to develop an efficient organization of labor through the time study of each technological process and to determine production units for each process.

After completion of this initial stage, it would be my responsibility to assist in the implementation of similar labor organization throughout all the factories in the Ukraine, which our office oversaw.

In a short time period I became acquainted with the colleagues from the other departments and with the management. The Director of the company was an old Bolshevik by the name Ivan Vinokashnev. He was not college educated, but very energetic, bright individual, and was on friendly terms with the employees. He demanded discipline, honesty and a good attitude from his staff. He believed this would make it easier for everyone to accomplish their professional duties.

There were a number of young people, several years out of college, working in the department with me. Soon I became friendly with most of them.

I was often traveling on business to the different factories, meeting many people. I educated them how they could improve efficiency in their production. Slowly, but surely, I earned my coworkers respect and good reputation for my analytical skills, and established many important professional contacts.

One day, at the beginning of 1937, I came to work and found out that our Director, Mr. Vinokashnev, was arrested. He was declared *an enemy of the Soviet people.* The news affected not just me, but all of the employees. Nobody could believe that something like this was possibly true.

We all knew Mr. Vinokashnev as a very decent, hardworking and honest man. We could not imagine that an old Bolshevik like him could be considered a threat to anyone. Nobody dared to express their thoughts out loud, only shared them in small groups of close friends. Everyone was afraid to receive a similar fate for discussing the matter. Within a few days his deputy was arrested as well.

Our company was experiencing some of its darkest days. No one acted normally, and people were beginning to lose their trust in each other. Wild rumors would surface and fade within the same day, concerning different people. We all were brainwashed during special political meetings.

Everyone was asked to reveal the names of the individuals, who were *enemies* of the Soviet people, and who penetrated into the leadership positions in our society. We were told that people like that are in almost every family, and that they want to destroy our socialist system. Life at work was becoming a nightmare.

Coworkers did not talk to one another. Nobody expressed any distaste or praise for the work of the others. Everyone kept their opinions to themselves, so as not to arouse the scrutinizing eyes of the Communist Party leaders.

I myself was very frightened. My brothers Levi and Tsezar both held high level positions. They could have been easily arrested by the testimony of a jealous or disgruntled coworker.

It was a horrifying time, because people like me were unable to help others or themselves. We were told that we must watch each other in order to report any and all suspicious persons to the authorities, and let the authorities dealt with them.

Soon a new company Director, Mr. Aaron Kagan, was appointed. His new deputy became Mr. Felix Umansky. The new Director gave us the impression that he was an ordinary man. He did not have an education beyond high school, nor any outstanding characteristics, or talents.

His deputy, Mr. Umansky, showed more initiative and energy in trying to normalize the working environment. He immediately enforced strict discipline, and requested a private meeting with each employee, to get acquainted with everyone.

As time went on, our company got back on its feet and the working environment became somewhat normal. The responsibilities of our company were broadened, and we grew in size to meet industrial demand. We now oversaw not only regional and republican footwear factories, but also the factories that supplied raw materials, to be used in footwear production.

The Ministry of Light Industry restructured our company and created a new one, which now oversaw all factories related to the leather manufacturing and footwear production industry in the Ukraine Republic. During restructuring, several employees, including myself, were transferred to the new company. I was appointed a Manager in the Department of Labor and Wages.

My new boss was an old Bolshevik, Civil War veteran, named Mr. Tokarsky. He was an invalid, missing one of his legs, from combat actions during the Civil War. He did not have the proper experience as an administrator.

Our Chief Engineer was hired fresh out of college with a total lack of industrial experience. He had little respect for Mr. Tokarsky. When he talked with me or anyone else with job experience, we felt that he was very sure of himself. He had to let everyone know that no matter how good they might be at their individual task, he had the power and was charged to do everything his way. You could see certain disrespect in his eyes when older and more experienced employees would point out his shortcomings, and give him suggestions on how to avoid them.

I earned a great deal of respect from Mr. Tokarsky. Not only did he regularly ask my opinion on certain issues, he also shared with me his experience in dealing with the Chief Engineer. By nature Mr. Tokarsky was a kind and honest man, but with insufficient ability to manage a company. His disability made him physically weak.

He always sought advice from the experienced employees, and had good working relationships with the Directors of the factories, which our office oversaw. After consulting with several specialists, he tried to be firm in his decisions. It was difficult not to respect him for all the work he put into the company, and for his sincere desire to learn business. Unfortunately, his poor health was really starting to affect him, and in 1939 he quit.

Mr. Korofelov was selected by the Ministry of Light Industry to replace him. He was younger and had a prominent military career prior to being appointed to this position. He had good organizational skills and demanded personal respect from all his employees. He expected all his directives to be executed perfectly all the time. I am not sure exactly how, but I became one of the subordinates in the company who earned his respect.

He always invited me to the meetings and asked to accompany him on business trips to different factories. He never took *no* for an answer, and showed the Chief Engineer who was really in charge. Before issuing any executive order he would always seek my professional advice. He gained authority among the employees and worked in the company until the outbreak of the Great Patriotic War in June of 1941.

My professional career moved along very successfully and I enjoyed my work. I earned respect from people with whom I worked. With every business trip to an industrial site, I gained new knowledge in dealing with the latest technology and organization of labor. I also earned respect within the Ministry of Light Industry, and was always invited to the meetings, attended by the heads of various departments and industry leaders.

There were important discussions about the development of Light Industry in the Soviet Union. The Minister himself often made presentations at these meetings and shared knowledge and information he gained on the business trips abroad. My job was almost my entire life, although I still managed to have friends.

During this period my life was changing slowly, but surely. I still continued to correspond with Vladimir. We tried to be honest with one another, and wrote about almost anything that was going on in our lives. He was happy that my career was progressing so well. He told me that I deserved everything I worked for. Vladimir was close to completing his assignment in Artiomovsk, and planned to come back to Kiev.

For a while now one of my colleagues, Arkadi Koval, had been showing certain affection for me. He often telephoned me during the day with conversations outside of our professional responsibilities. This was not left without notice by the other employees.

One day Arkadi caught up with me after work, and walked me to my apartment. As time went on, he visited me more frequently. He invited me to the theaters, concerts and movies. Although he was nice with me, to others, especially at work, he was rude, self-centered and smug. This side of him I did not like. He was persistent, and it was extremely difficult to avoid him.

Once when he was visiting me, my old school friend, Manya Choletsky, stopped in. Manya was a modest beauty, but she was very bright, and had a great sense of humor. The three of us went out and had a wonderful evening. Arkadi volunteered to walk Manya home, and after that evening, his phone calls to me became less frequent. This made me somewhat concerned, even though I did not like him all that much. Still, it felt nice to have the attention.

Some time later, Manya came and told me that she and Arkadi had started seeing each other, and that she felt awkward in my presence. I replied that it did not bother me at all, and that she should not think twice about getting serious with Arkadi. I was not genuinely interested in him, and that he was all hers. I told her my impression of him at work, to make sure she was not just seeing the good side of him, and not the whole person.

About three months later, Manya and Arkadi were still dating each other. I asked her how their relationship progressed. Manya happily replied that Arkadi was giving her lots of affection, and their fondness for each other was growing stronger with every passing day. They were planning to get married. I was truly happy for her and wished them the best of luck.

The marriage fell apart, and within a year she left him. Later on Manya shared with me that Arkadi was very demanding and controlling, always insisting his smallest request was fulfilled without any questions. He often was rude and disrespectful towards her and she ran away from him. He followed and threatened her. She had to leave Kiev in order to escape from him. The marriage left bitter feelings in her heart, and she had trouble intrusting her life to any man in the future. She never married again.

My friendship with Manya remained strong for many years to come. I kept in touch with her all my life in the USSR and through correspondence after my emigration to the USA. She was always very affectionate towards my daughter.

I continued to meet and see different men, including my future husband. He gave me much attention and showed his sincere interest. The constant comparison I always had for every man against Vladimir, prevented me from making serious decisions. I did not usually show as much interest in men I met, as they did for me.

For a time I dated a man named Alexei Brodsky. He was a good-looking man and enjoyed music. Once on my date with him, we met some of my friends from work. The next day in the office, my friends joked that I was dating a much older man. Our age difference was only five years. After that I tried to avoid him.

I liked spending my free time with the friends from work more than anyone else. We had a nice group of young people and shared many common interests. We enjoyed each other's company and spent holidays together.

At the beginning of 1939, I received a letter from Vladimir. In the letter he said that several changes had occurred in his life, and he felt it was necessary to share them with me.

At his job in Artiomovsk, where he worked as a Manager of the Planning Department, was a young woman working in the chemical laboratory. They often had to resolve business issues. After a while, she began showing her affection for Vladimir. She showered him with lots of attention, and practically followed him wherever he went. He decided to talk to her and asked to stop pursuing him. He really did not have any feelings for her outside of a business context.

After he told her that, she broke down and began to cry. It became obvious that she had been in love with him for quite a while, and she could not handle his rejection. Vladimir tried to lessen the blow, saying that she was still young, and that she would find someone who truly deserves her love.

He also told her that he was in love with another woman, and that after completion of his job assignment he will be going back to Kiev. She broke down in tears and replied that she would forever love only him. Vladimir was very troubled by this situation. He requested to be transferred to another factory.

After reading the letter, I felt a certain degree of relief. The fact was that after graduation we worked in different cities. My feelings for Vladimir were never more than of great friendship and respect. I felt at ease with myself. I sat down to write a letter, and put thoughts into what I wanted to say. I knew it might push Vladimir out of my life forever.

In the letter I said, it was fate that brought this woman into his life. He should respect her deep feelings. I believed he knew what it meant to love. This was no coincidence that he was pulled away from me, and pushed towards this woman. I felt that she truly loved him, and that it would be best for him to be with her.

In the letter I told Vladimir that he was a man who deserved to be loved. He would find happiness with this young woman. I could never marry outside of my Jewish faith. Distance separating us was only hastening the inevitable. I told that he was free to do what was best for him. I was adamant that it would be better now to go on with his life, rather than to wait for something that could never happen.

I asked Vladimir not to return from Artiomovsk, but instead spend more time with the young woman, so that they could become better acquainted with each other. The best years of our lives were passing by. I wished him to be happy, before it was too late.

A year after, I received a letter from the young woman. She was writing that they both had read my letter, and Vladimir was learning to let go of me. She wanted to thank me, and promised that she would try to make him happy.

I felt relieved that the situation between the three of us worked out the way it did. Although it might not be considered the happiest of endings, we received what was deep down the best for each of us.

I celebrated the New Year of 1940 in the company of my friends. At the party I met a young man. His name was Grisha. He was quite skilled in playing the violin and provided great entertainment for our company. He had very nice manners and the way he presented himself to me.

He was dressed very modestly, but neatly. Grisha worked as a Secretary of the Science Department in the Ministry of High Education. After the party was over, he invited everyone to come visit him. Grisha gave everybody his business phone number and home address. Rarely someone had a telephone at home in those days.

Two months after the New Year's party, I occasionally met him in downtown Kiev, where his office was located. He saw me and remembered who I was. He struck up a conversation and asked why I did not call or visit him. Grisha told me that almost everyone else had seen him after the New Year's party, except me. I replied that I did not like to call young men on my own initiative, and we parted again.

In the summer of 1940, my school friend, Frida Weytzman, visited me. After high school she went on to graduate from the Aviation Technology Institute in Moscow. There she met a man, Yuri Goncharov, whom she later married. She was a very beautiful young woman and turned out to be very successful in an engineering career dominated by men. After graduation, Frida and her husband received a job offer in the same city, about 2000 miles away from Moscow.

On their way to a new place and a new life, they stopped to visit friends. One of them was an old flame, Frida had much earlier in her life. They got along extremely well. Frida's husband became jealous, and told her to stop flirting. He reminded her that she was his wife now.

Frida got upset and angered that Yuri did not trust her. She was carrying his baby. Frida loved her husband dearly, and she was just having a conversation with an old friend.

This seemed innocent enough in her eyes. Frida decided to teach Mike a lesson, and forced an apology out of him.

She wrote a letter to her brother, asking him to come and get her. She left for Kiev without her husband. Frida was sure that after a while Yuri would come begging for her to take him back, and apologized for not trusting her. Her plans did not quite go as she had hoped.

Some time later, Frida gave birth to a baby girl. She had a complicated delivery and was very weak. She never in her life heard from Yuri again. All the care for the new baby and young mother fell on the shoulders of Frida's brother and sisters. They rented an apartment for her, and as soon as she was strong enough, she found an engineering position at a Kiev Aviation Plant.

There she met a man, who fell in love with her. His family expressly forbade him from marrying a woman with a child. He married another woman and later on they divorced. He never found true love and spent the rest of his life alone.

One day I met Frida downtown after work, and we walked together to her apartment. I wanted to see her little daughter and the place she lived in. On the way to her apartment, two young men, Grisha and his friend, stopped us. We walked together to Frida's place, and then they walked me home.

Before departing, Grisha asked if he could call me sometimes. I replied *yes* and gave him my business phone number. Shortly thereafter, he called me and asked if I would like to get together with him and his friend. I agreed, and later on that evening the three of us had a wonderful time. From then on, his phone calls became frequent, and we spent most of our free time together. He never came to see me without flowers. My fondness for him grew stronger with every passing day.

Grisha's job demanded him to work long hours. I always questioned what a man like him saw in me. I was such an ordinary beauty. What possibly could have attracted him to me? This just never seemed like it was real.

Frida, on the other hand, thought we were perfect for each other. When we talked, I would sometimes say that I thought he was too good for me. She would just get mad at me for saying that. Frida told me that I had an inner beauty like no one else. Men fell in love with my charisma and my character. She said it took decent man like Grisha to appreciate me. I would always laugh at that.

In the winter of 1941, my sister Tsilya with her husband and two children celebrated a special occasion. They received a large three-room apartment through the company where her husband worked. The apartment was just for one family, with no neighbors to share a bathroom or kitchen.

This was a very happy occasion and they decided to throw a big party. They invited all the members of our large family and their friends to celebrate. I came to the party with Grisha and introduced him to my family. I fell in love with him as we continued dating.

We both had a wonderful time at the party. He felt at ease around my family, and everybody liked him. We continued dating, and in May of 1941, Grisha proposed to me. He told me that he liked my independent character, my sincere soul, and my ability to understand and share his interests. I was caught unprepared by this, to say the least. I was a bit confused by the sudden rush of emotions, but then a warm feeling passed throughout my body. We hugged and kissed each other. We decided to get married in the fall.

GREAT PATRIOTIC WAR 1941-1945

June 22, 1941, was a beautiful summer Sunday. Grisha and I were planning to go for the opening ceremony of a newly built sport stadium. We were looking forward to a wonderful weekend together.

Early in the morning, I was awakened by the loud bursts of noise. This was the sound of exploding bombs. We heard an announcement on the radio that Germany had declared unprovoked war on the Soviet Union. That day changed our lives forever in a way we never could foresee.

Every citizen had strong patriotic feelings of duty to defend our beloved Motherland. The majority of working population went to the places of their employment. Each of us was ready to do whatever would be required. Everybody was sent home to wait for further instructions.

Later on the same day Grisha and I met. The sadness in his eyes made me shiver. He told me that the war would be protracted. The Soviet Union was not prepared for the unexpected German attack the way government officials tried to present the situation to the public. Many prominent military leaders and army officers were executed or imprisoned during Joseph Stalin's *Great Purge*. He was concerned that the Red Army would suffer tremendous losses.

This was by far the grimmest day we had ever spent together. We never discussed what we both knew was going to happen. Unfortunately, it happened much faster than we had thought.

The following day Grisha called me with the news. He had received a telegram from the local military recruitment office, and was instructed to appear there on the date stated in the telegram. I still did not fully realize what all this meant and all the horrors that this war would bring to our lives. Everything was happening so suddenly that my mind could not keep up with my heart.

I patiently waited for Grisha after he had gone to the military recruitment office. Awful thoughts were running through my mind. I thought of him and what was awaiting us. He finally called and told me that the local recruitment officer had instructed him not to go to work the following day, and wait for new orders.

My naiveté told me that it was the right thing to do: go and fight the Germans, and to defend our country against Nazi occupation. I told Grisha that serving in the Red Army was duty of every able man. I thought that Germans would be defeated and quickly pushed out of the USSR. I did not truly understand the reality and cruelty of the war and neither did Grisha. We would both pay a high price for our patriotic feelings of duty to serve and protect our Motherland.

At the outbreak of the war, the civilian population continued reporting to work every day, even though nobody could really work. Everybody was discussing events and news that were rapidly changing. At the very end of June all able employees were sent to the outskirts of Kiev to dig antitank trenches. Working away from the city, we were not sure what was going on there. Information we were receiving was very sporadic.

At the same time evacuation of vital industry and civilian population to the remote regions of the USSR began. Ration cards system was introduced.

On July 5, 1941, when I returned to Kiev, I witnessed a frightening picture of panic. Everybody was in a hurry searching for salvation, trying to flee the city, which soon would be occupied by the Germans. When I reached our apartment, I saw that we had a new family member living with us. Before I left to dig trenches, our household consisted of my mother, father, brother Michael and I. Now we had my brother Tsezar's mother-in-law living with us.

I asked father what had happened? He explained that Tsezar's wife Dora brought her mother and a package of food. She told my parents that the Germans were not going to harm older people, and that they could stay in Kiev. She left her mother with my parents. Dora also brought a box of family valuables for safekeeping. Tsezar with the family were evacuating to the city of Kharkov[7]. His office was in the process of transferring employees and their families there.

I was amazed by my sister-in-law's actions, and the fact that she made a decision about our parents' well-being. My sister Tsilya and her two small children were also preparing for the evacuation to Kharkov.

My brother Levi with his family were preparing for the evacuation to Novosibirsk, a city in Siberia. He held a key level position in the plant, which manufactured planes. Levi was placed in charge of the personnel and equipment evacuation.

---

7 Kharkov is about 310 miles northeast of Kiev.

My sister Roza was still in Kiev. She was awaiting her son, Abraham, who was a student in the Institute of Structural Engineering and Architecture. He was completing internship in the city of Zhitomir, about 85 miles from Kiev. I went to see Roza and her husband. They informed me that Grisha was visiting them almost every day, asking about me.

Rosa told me that Tsezar was still in Kiev. I decided to see my brother. We had a very serious conversation, and I warned him that if he was not going to help evacuate our parents and his mother-in-law, I would stay in Kiev with them. I told him that whatever happened to us would be on his conscience[8]. He promised to do everything in his power to help.

The next day I went to my office and learned that the greater part of the employees had already been evacuated to the city of Kuibishev, in the Russian heartland, on the Volga River. Only the Deputy Director and Personnel Manager were still in Kiev. They handled all necessary paper work, required for the employees and their families' evacuation to the remote region of the country.

I went to the Personnel Department and was told that my evacuation documents would be processed expediently. In the evening I met with Grisha. He did not have a specific destination to report to. He was concerned that my parents, my disabled brother and I were still in Kiev. He tried to cheer me up, even though he was very sad.

On July 9, I met my old college friend. We conversed about current events, and she told me that her husband would be evacuating with the family. I was surprised to hear that her husband was allowed to evacuate. All able men of his age

---

8 Kiev was occupied by Germans on September 19, 1941. On September 29-30, 1941, SS and German police murdered in Babi Yar the Jewish population of Kiev, who did not flee.

were called to active duty. My friend explained that because she received proper evacuation documents at her place of employment, her husband was taken off active duty list, and received permission to evacuate with the family.

I went immediately to the Personnel Department at my place of work. The Personnel Manager was still there. I asked him to include Grisha's name in my evacuation documents, and he agreed. I hurried to see my sister Roza and shared the good news with her. I wrote a note to Grisha, asking him immediately to come to my sister's apartment. Roza's domestic helper, Galya, went to deliver my note. Grisha was not home.

He came to see us in the evening, and I told him about what I learned from my friend. Grisha took all the evacuation documents that were issued for me, with his name included. He promised that the next morning he would go to the military recruitment office.

On July 10, 1941, he presented all the documents to the officer in charge. In reply, Grisha was told that it was a bit too late. New orders came in from the Regional Military Office, prohibiting the evacuation of anybody who was able to serve.

We both were devastated by this news. I blamed myself, for not knowing the rules, and not acting sooner. I felt that I did not do everything in my power to save his life, due to my unawareness and beliefs that it was his duty to serve. I was in a dreadful mood.

Tsezar kept his promise. He secured all the documents required for the evacuation of our parents and his mother-in-law. I helped to pack their bare necessities, took them to the railroad station, and put on a train to Kharkov.

I stayed behind in Kiev, waiting for Roza's family. I intended to evacuate with them. Her son finally arrived home. He was issued required documents for evacuation to the city of Kuibishev with all the students attending Institute of Structural Engineering and Architecture. Instead, he decided to enlist in the Red Army.

On the last day of work, I was given my "Employment History Book" and other documents, required for the evacuation. I was very depressed, not knowing what awaited us ahead. I was standing in my office near the window looking down on the street, watching people carrying suitcases with their belongings, in a hurry to leave Kiev.

All of a sudden, one of my colleagues walked towards me. His name was Boris. He told me that for a long time he was afraid to approach and express his feelings for me. As we were leaving, without knowing what would happen to us, he got his courage to tell, he was in love with me.

He asked for permission to write me. He also hoped that I would reply. Boris wanted to give me address of his parents in Siberia. There was no paper to write on. He wrote their address on the back cover of my "Employment History Book." He asked me to write to his parents and to find out if he was alive or dead. I got very emotional and did not know what to say. I wished him well and said that I hoped everything would be all right. Tears ran down my cheeks as we hugged each other goodbye.

The next morning I left Kiev for Kharkov with my sister Roza and her husband Tevi. Tsezar arranged a car for us and we arrived to Kharkov before our parents. I was able to meet them at the railroad station and they were very happy. We all were settled in the dormitory of the "Tractor Plant." A large number of people were sharing the same rooms. Nobody complained about lack of privacy.

The next day I went to the factory, where I was assigned for evacuation. I met Director and Controller from our office there. Together we were working on the final report of the Ukraine footwear industry evacuation. After this task was completed, both men went to the District Military Office and were directed to report to active duty. I was left in charge of the second stage footwear industry evacuation, from Kharkov to the specified destinations in the depth of Russia.

In Kharkov, the state of war was felt even stronger then in Kiev. The city was bombarded several times every day. Many buildings were destroyed and there were a large number of casualties among the civilian population. Our factory was frequently bombarded and we all ran outside and watched the fire and exploding bombs.

On September 16, 1941, I received last letter from Grisha. He gave me his military field address and said that soon they will be leaving Kiev. On September 19, 1941, Kiev was occupied by German troops.

I sent numerous letters to Grisha's military field address. I received no reply from him. The only letter, which I received from this address, stated that his whereabouts was unknown. I could only assume that he might got in the harm's way between September 16 and September 19 of 1941.

Life in Kharkov was becoming more dangerous with every passing day. Two of my sisters, Roza and Tsilya with their families, and Tsezar's wife Dora, with their son, were evacuated from Kharkov to Tashkent, capital of the Uzbek Republic. My parents with disabled brother Michael, and mother of my sister-in-law were directed to be evacuated from Kharkov to Saratov, a city on the Volga River.

Our family separation was heartbreaking for all and especially for my elderly parents. To get tickets on the train was very difficult. Everybody tried to flee Kharkov as soon as possible. The frequency of the bombardments increased and the number of civilian casualties grew tremendously.

The factory I was assigned to was directed to be evacuated to the city of Sverdlovsk[9], a large industrial center in the Ural region. All the production equipment was sent to the footwear factory there.

I was unable to leave the factory where I was registered for evacuation. This was very dangerous. I wanted to be with my parents and brother. I decided that as soon as I would arrive in Sverdlovsk, I would resign my position and ask for my transfer to a footwear factory in Saratov. I gave all my warm clothing to my parents and was left with a trench coat and a pair of shoes. Later on I very much regretted my lack of practical sense.

Our train ride to the city of Sverdlovsk[10] was long and dangerous. We often had to get off the train to hide from the German planes that followed us. One day during our journey, the train was stopped for refueling. We were told that we would have about two hours of free time.

Many people left the train to get a breath of fresh air, to wash and to buy some food. Returning back to the train, we heard a very loud explosion and saw fire and smoke coming out. We ran away to find out what was going on.

We were told that German planes threw firebombs on our train and sections of it were burned to the ground. A large number of people lost their lives. Our section of the train was not damaged. We were on the road for almost three

---

9 Sverdlovsk is presently Yekaterinburg.
10 Distance between Kharkov and Sverdlovsk is approximately 1372 miles.

exhausting weeks, and arrived in Sverdlovsk at the beginning of November.

On arrival, evacuees were settled in the dormitory, which belonged to the factory "Ural Shoes." We lived there for several months. Later on we were resettled among the employees of the factory.

Nina, a woman from Leningrad and I, were settled in the apartment, which belonged to the woman named Galya. Her husband was serving in the Red Army. She had two rooms and lived now by herself. One of the rooms was given to us. Galya was not very happy with this arrangement, but was unable to change anything in these dire circumstances. Soon she got used to the new way of life.

The apartment building was very close to the factory where I was assigned to work. It took me only ten minutes to walk there. That really saved my life, since I did not have warm clothing or winter boots. Winters in the Ural region were prolonged and very cold.

I worked in the position of Industrial Engineer. Our lives were a big struggle to survive one day at a time. Each employee received a daily food rationing card for a pound and a quarter of bread. In the factory cafeteria we were able to buy noodle soup, made without any fat. During these times, we thought that bread was very tasty, and ate it piece by piece before dinner. For dinner we went to the cafeteria and ate noodle soup.

In spite of hard times, nobody complained. Everybody understood that it was wartime. Many people suffered considerably more then us.

My roommate Nina was much older than I. We became really good friends and shared whatever small possessions we had. She tried to help me with warm clothing and winter boots. Each of us had a sister in Leningrad, which was under the German Siege[11].

After graduation from college, Etya was offered an engineering position with the large industrial complex in Leningrad. She accepted an offer and now was trapped in the city. Leningrad's population was suffering from cold and hunger. Loss of lives was tremendous, especially among the old and very young. Etya miraculously survived through the nine hundred days of the siege. The city was never surrendered to the Germans, and after the war was awarded the title of Hero City.

I shared with Nina worries about my parents and all my extended family. I tried to find ways to get in touch with them. My brother Levi and his wife were in Novosibirsk. Levi was working at the Aviation Plant. He was a Manager of the Purchasing Department. This was a position of high responsibility. I wrote him a letter and we met in Sverdlovsk, where he came on business. At the time of our meeting, he told me what had happened to our parents during the evacuation from Kharkov to Saratov. This story broke my heart.

My father sent Levi a letter. He described that their train never reached Saratov, which was their final destination. Everybody was asked to get off the train in the village of Makrous, Saratov region. Each person able to work was assigned a job at one of the collective farms in the region.

My elderly parents with a disabled brother and frail mother of my sister-in-law were settled in a hut. The winter was very cold and severe winds made their existence even more difficult to endure. Snow was so deep that it reached almost to the roof of the hut and it was cold inside. There was no running water.

---

11 Siege of Leningrad started on September 8, 1941 and was lifted on January 27, 1944.

My parents had to go to the river and break a hole in the ice in order to get a bucket of water.

My seventy-year-old father was assigned a job of night security guard at the barn. He was a sole provider of the scarce food supply for the family. He was issued a food rationing card for four people. My mother was his main helper.

After I learned what happened to our parents, I insisted that Levi go to Makrous village and bring them to Novosibirsk, where he could help them to survive. Regrettably, he was unable to secure release documents from his employer, required to travel across the country during the war. At the time, his presence was essential at the plant, which supplied military planes for the front. Levi gave me Roza's family address in Tashkent.

I decided to travel to Makrous village by myself, and get our parents out of these horrible living conditions. My roommate Nina insisted that it would be very dangerous for me to do it on my own. She suggested that my brothers would have to take this upon themselves in order to rescue our parents.

I sent letters to my brother Tsezar and my brother-in-law Tevi. I told that if they would not help our parents, I would be forced to risk my life and go on my own.

Travel on the trains was very difficult during the war. Each train was loaded beyond capacity to transport wounded, evacuees, supplies and equipment. To get a ticket for travel by train during wartime required special permission. Tsezar was on active duty. He secured all the required documents for Tevi.

Tevi, with great difficulties, risking his life, was eventually able to get to Makrous village. He witnessed that each family member suffered from frostbites and hunger. With a tremendous effort he brought all four of them to Tashkent. They would not survive otherwise. That was a heroic act during the war. I was grateful to Tevi for his devotion and sacrifice all my life.

Later on I learned more details from my sister Tsilya. She stopped in Sverdlovsk to see me en route to her husband. Tsilya told me what really had happened to our parents and why they never reached Saratov.

My father was a man of great courage and strong will. He was in charge of the family's welfare, and took care of all their needs. He also tried to act as a cheerleader in these tragic circumstances. On one of the scheduled stops, he got off the train to find and buy some food and water. When he returned the train was already gone.

Due to unforeseen circumstances, the train departed earlier and my father was left alone at the railroad station. He went to see the station manager and explained that two elderly women and a disabled young man were left on the train without anybody who could help them. The station manager initiated a search along the railroad route for this specific train and found its location.

My father was given ground transportation to catch this train. When he finally met with the family they were sad and distressed. This was a miracle during the period of complete chaos that they were able to reunite.

Later on during their journey, the order came to take everybody off the train in the village of Makrous, in the Saratov region. My elderly father accepted a job of the security guard at the barn with the cows and horses. He would not be issued the ration card to feed his family, otherwise.

The barn was situated not far from the woods. One night when my father was on duty, the hungry wolves, looking for food, approached very close towards the fence surrounding the animals. Father was alone, but he did not panic. He began to throw large pieces of burning wood, and then started a campfire, using straw, which served as food for the cows and horses. He fought with the wolves till sunrise.

After this incident my mother insisted that he quit his job, and went to the District Military Authority to ask for help. My father was able to arrange an appointment with the officer in charge and gave him the name of his oldest son, Tsezar. Tsezar was on active duty with the Army Corps of Engineers. An officer got in touch with the division where my brother served. Soon after that my father received a certificate, authorizing him to receive a small monetary allowance, enough to survive their day-to-day existence.

The process of filling out required paperwork was very difficult for my father. He was almost illiterate. He needed help to properly fill out an application and other required documents. Thanks to his tremendous energy and perseverance, our loved ones were able to survive.

After I learned about our parents' heartrending existence, I decided to do whatever it took to reunite the family. We were all scattered around a vast country. Nobody knew how long the war would last and what would be the outcome. Living apart we were unable to help each other morally, physically and financially.

I wrote a letter to my brother Levi in Novosibirsk. I asked for his help with my employment and securing all the required documents for my transfer from Sverdlovsk to Novosibirsk. I was single, had a solid work experience, numerous awards, honors and commendations in my "Employment History Book." I sent all the documents to Novosibirsk. Very soon I received an offer to work at the same Aviation Plant where

Levi was working. They needed someone with an industrial engineering background.

Now my task was to get a release from the factory in Sverdlovsk. That was not easy. The Director of the factory did not want to sign my release. My friends helped to convince him that it was necessary for me to reunite with the family. After some negotiations he finally agreed. I was given a warm farewell. My friends helped me to get to the railroad station and put me on the train.

For many years I continued my correspondence with the friends whom I met in Sverdlovsk. People born and raised in the Ural region were much more conservative and humble compared to those who came during evacuation from the European part of the Soviet Union. At the same time they were sincere, honest and possessed high tenacity. Life in Sverdlovsk left sweet memories of those bitter times.

In 1943 I arrived in Novosibirsk. I settled with my brother Levi and his wife Eva. Levi was devastated with the horrific news. His only son, Naum, who just turned twenty years old, enlisted to serve in the Red Army. Naum had a strong conviction of duty to defend his beloved Motherland. My brother and his wife Eva received a letter informing that their son was listed as missing in action.

Levi suffered tremendously from this loss. He worked very long hours. When he returned home from work late at night, he was unable to sleep. He lost weight and looked like a very old man.

In this situation I was unable to ask my brother for help in bringing our parents from Tashkent to Novosibirsk. I knew that I had to secure an apartment for myself. Only then would I be able to bring our parents and disabled brother to live with me.

At the Aviation Plant I accepted the position of Manager in the Division of Planes Assembly and Release. I was new to the aviation industry. Manufacturing processes were completely different from the industry I had worked in before.

The division I was assigned to work for had its own airfield, where planes were tested prior to final acceptance and release by the military inspectors. I had eight people under my direct supervision. My main objective was to reduce costs associated with the plane production. Achieving this goal required the reduction of the high scrap rate from parts that did not meet engineering specifications.

I understood that in order to be able to accomplish my goal, I had to acquire a good knowledge of each technological process and to identify areas where the high scrap rate was generated. The largest part of the work force at the plant were women and teenagers. They replaced workers who were called to active duty. Only areas of the highest importance and responsibilities employed well qualified and experienced workers.

In our division, military personnel inspected planes for acceptance. The majority of the officers were young men. Among them was one woman.

I became friendly with the Manager of the Planes Acceptance Group. l explained that this industry was new to me and asked his permission to be present during the plane inspection. He gave me his *okay*.

I asked the inspecting officer to explain the criteria for parts rejection or acceptance. The officer described what is considered an acceptable part and what is considered a defect. I helped him to fill in rejection reports.

The first month of my employment was spent mostly on the production floor, studying the manufacturing processes.

I learned how parts were made and what constituted a defect. I familiarized myself with almost every storage area, where each plane was numbered and had a list of the itemized components attached.

For the parts, which deviated from the engineering specification, additional tools and materials were used to replace them. That required approval from the technical department. I familiarized myself with the work of the departments, which supplied our department with the components for the plane assembly.

I learned the specifics of the job performed by each individual in my department. Some of the workers were not very friendly towards me. I was given a job and had to do it the best way I knew how. I stayed late at work, after everybody from my department had left. I studied all the documents, which were delivered to the department during the day and analyzed them.

With the fresh look at the new industry and with my experience in the organization of labor, I was able to identify several problems. I shared my findings with the military inspector. He was surprised that I was able to learn so much in such a short time. He decided to help me develop a plan for improved productivity in the specific manufacturing areas.

I also went to the Manager of the Technical Department. Together we looked at each deviation in the technological process. I instructed coworkers in my department that no additional materials or tools would be released without my signature, and that all the salvage orders requests would be given to me for approval.

I developed a plan for the improvements and costs reductions in the labor and materials. This plan was submitted to the Division Manager. He reviewed my proposal, made several corrections and approved it.

From that time my *real* work began. I was young, and had a desire to learn. I put all energy and knowledge into my work. I felt strongly that the Red Army victory in the war against Germany depended greatly on the high quality planes, which our plant manufactured.

As a result of the changes introduced by me, we achieved significant reduction in the cost per plane. I had earned my coworkers respect, not only in my department, but from the other departments as well. I was given more responsibilities.

The main reason for my transfer to Novosibirsk from Sverdlovsk was to bring my parents from Tashkent and to reunite our family. I did not have my own apartment in Novosibirsk and continued to stay temporarily with my brother Levi and his wife.

The plant, where I worked, had more then twenty thousands employees. It was located in the suburb of the city. The largest number of the personnel lived in the apartment buildings built for the employees in the nearby town. Several apartment buildings were built in the city for the plant management. My brother lived in one of the apartment buildings in the city.

One year after I was hired and earned respect from the management, I approached the Division Manager with the request to help me secure my own apartment. With his help, through our Personnel Department, I was approved to receive one room in the apartment building in the city. The room was fairly big. Finally, I would be able to reunite our family. I was in a hurry to do that. My father sent me a letter, saying that mother was very weak.

I was approved for the business trip to Tashkent, and secured all the required documents for travel across the country during wartime. My brother Levi spent long hours at work. He continued to suffer terribly from the loss of his only son. There was nobody who could help me get to the train station. Public transportation was not available, and I walked along with my luggage.

I did not realize that I was not strong enough, and it took me longer then I thought it should to get to the station. The train was supposed to leave shortly. I still did not have a ticket, which was reserved for me. Inside the station I had to go to the reservation office to receive it. Nobody with luggage was allowed to enter this office.

I asked a stranger sitting at the bench if he would watch my luggage while I went to get a ticket. After I returned, the young man who was watching my luggage got up and offered me a seat. He was surprised that during these tumultuous times I left my suitcases with a stranger. I replied that I had good intuition and felt that he could be trusted. He had just helped his friend to get on the train. By shear coincidence, he was still at the station when I showed up.

His name was Michael. We talked for a little bit before my train arrived. I told him the reason I was going to Tashkent. He asked for my address and if he could meet with me after my return. Michael helped me to get on the train and promised to send a telegram to my parents.

The journey to Tashkent was long and tiresome[12]. When I arrived, nobody met me at the railroad station. I thought that Michael probably never sent a telegram. I got a taxicab, and finally arrived at my parents' place. They were delighted to see me. Michael's telegram was delivered the next day.

We started preparing for the long journey from Middle Asia to Siberia. My mother was very weak. While we were

---

12 Distance between Novosibirsk and Tashkent is about 1137 miles.

packing, she fell on the floor. She had a stroke and died the next day with a clear mind, but unable to speak. Her eyes expressed all the pain and sadness, which she felt. Her death brought great sorrow to all of us and completely changed our plans.

Roza and father did not want to leave Tashkent immediately after our mother's death. My time off from work was coming to an end. The decision was made that only my brother-in-law would be going to Novosibirsk with me. His first order of business would be to find a suitable employment. After he was settled, the rest of the family would come.

When Tevi and I returned to Novosibirsk, Eva met us at the train station. She told me that the young man, who I met at the railroad station, visited them several times and inquired about me. I did not pay any attention to this news. I was mourning the death of my mother.

I returned to work quite depressed. Many important issues were waiting for my decision and I completely immersed myself in my work. Within two days after my return to Novosibirsk, I received a notice in the mail from Michael. He scheduled time for a long distance telephone conversation with me.

He was unable to wait until I would be back from Tashkent and had to leave on a business trip to Krasnoyarsk[13]. Michael told me that he would like to stay in touch and asked to write down the name and address of his sister in Novosibirsk. I did not feel at ease to visit someone I never met before. My sister-in-law Eva offered to go with me.

One weekend we decided to visit Michael's sister. Her name was Lisa. She was a beautiful young woman and was very pleased to meet with us. Lisa introduced us to her husband

13 Krasnoyarsk is a third largest city in Siberia.

and brother-in-law, who lived with them. Her brother-in-law was a handsome young man. He was tall, broad-shouldered and looked strong. His name was Senya.

When we were ready to leave, he offered to walk us home. As we approached my brother's apartment building, Eva invited us for a tea. We spent some time with her. I walked Senya to the door, and before departing he asked permission to visit with us next weekend. I agreed to meet him again.

After this meeting he continued to visit us every weekend. We went to the theaters, concerts and movies together. Senya was charismatic and easygoing. He was not very fond of Michael and considered him to be a womanizer. I did not pay much attention to his words. I did not consider this entire situation serious, and only looked at it as a chance to have good times on weekends.

Michael called me several more times, promising that his business plans might permit him to stop and see me in Novosibirsk. Evidently, such a possibility never arrived. We did not see each other again.

Senya dated me till the end of the war. I never gave him hope to think about our relationship as more than a friendship. I told him about Grisha, about my plans to return to Kiev as soon as the war was over and try to find him. Senya was a considerate man with the good manners. He cheered me up and said that one should never give up hope. This made our relationship easy to continue with no commitments towards each other.

At the beginning of 1944, Tevi went back to Tashkent and brought Roza, my father and brother to Novosibirsk. Dora's mother stayed in Tashkent with her. Everybody settled with me in one room. The living arrangements were not desirable for all of us. We decided to partition my room into two

72

separate rooms. My father, brother and I in one, and my sister with her husband in the other.

When I lived by myself, I did not have any problem with food. Our plant was in a privileged situation, because we manufactured planes for the front. I spent the whole day at work and received dinner in the cafeteria. There were several cafeterias throughout the plant, for different categories of employees: hourly, salaried and management.

When my family arrived, I was faced with the problem of how to provide for them. Our ration cards supplied us with very limited quantities of food, with almost no meat, butter, vegetables or fruits.

The main source of food in Siberia was potatoes. I was provided with a small plot of land by the plant, and we planted potatoes. Several times I went to a nearby village to exchange clothing, which Roza sewed, for meat, milk and eggs. I tried very hard to provide my loved ones with food, so that they would not go hungry.

One day I met my friend Frida. We were delighted to see each other. She evacuated with the Kiev Aviation Plant to Novosibirsk. We both were working at the same huge plant and did not meet before. She lived with the families of her two sisters. Their husbands were serving in the Red Army.

Sisters were helping Frida to take care of her little daughter. She had a very difficult life raising a child by herself, especially during the war. Frida was always a very generous person. She shared with me any food that she was able to exchange for clothing or other necessities in the village.

After the family was reunited and settled, I worked longer hours and tried to find out how to achieve even more improvements in the organization of labor and quality of the products. My state of mind reminded me of the time when

I was a college student. Whenever I had to solve a difficult mathematical problem, I was unable to fall asleep until the solution was found. I was working tirelessly all the time, trying to understand all the aspects of the task assigned to me.

Finally, measurable results were achieved. For the first half of the fiscal year, our division was able to be right on target, without exceeding expenses, and for the second half of the year, under budget.

My achievements were recognized. I received a monetary award. My picture was taken and posted on the plant "Wall of Honor." The plant employed over twenty thousands people and only about a hundred were bestowed with such a great honor.

The selection process among employees, whose candidacy was submitted for recognition, was very thorough. I was able to pass on every score. I could hardly believe, that for two years of my work at the plant, I became a famous and respected individual. Everybody congratulated me on my achievements. Now my goal was to keep up with the results.

Commander in Chief of the Red Army, Joseph Stalin, was in constant communication with the Director of the Aviation Plant through the direct telephone line. When Stalin called with the request to increase planes production, each plant division held a meeting. Stalin's personal appeal was a great morale booster. Every employee stayed at work as long as was required to complete assigned production quotas.

In the areas where the shortage of workers was especially critical, engineers and managers were helping to fill the gap. Patriotic feelings were on a very high level. War touched the lives of every employee and their families. Everybody wanted to achieve a victory over Germany.

At last the long awaited news arrived on May 9, 1945. On the radio all over the country was proclaimed that Germany signed an unconditional surrender. The war in Europe was finally over.

Nobody was required to work that day. Everybody ran to the streets. It is difficult to describe the joy and exultation experienced by all. Strangers hugged and kissed each other. Everybody greeted, hugged and kissed people in military uniforms and threw flowers at them. Every face shined with a smile and some with tears. For the moment, the Soviet people tried to forget personal losses, hardships and the price we all paid to witness this day. Everybody was united with the glory of victory over Nazi Germany.

All that came back later, when the fireworks stopped. The Soviet people paid a very heavy price for the victory. There was no single family who did not lose a loved one. Millions of people lost their lives or became disabled. Cities, towns and villages were destroyed. People lost the roofs over their heads and most of their possessions. The country infrastructure was shuttered.

Despite all the devastation and sufferings, victory revived a new desire to survive and live normal productive life. Those who were evacuated during the war to the remote regions of the USSR planned to return home. Everybody knew about the difficulties, which were awaiting them, but there was no force to stop people from going back home. *Reverse evacuation* began.

In our family, my brother Lazar, his wife and two daughters were the first who returned to Kiev. The neighbors, with whom they shared an apartment for twenty years before the war, occupied their three rooms. They immediately vacated these rooms.

That apartment served as an anchor for the return of the other family members to Kiev. It was the only apartment that survived bombardments and was still intact. The next family to arrive and settled with Lazar's family was my sister Tsilya, her husband and three children. Her husband was an officer in the Red Army. He was discharged with honors from military service and returned to begin work on the restoration of the city buildings and infrastructure.

LIFE AFTER THE WAR

After the war ended, I decided to return to Kiev and use all my energy to find Grisha. At that time, it was not allowed to simply leave your employer and move to another city. Special request for transfer or business trip document, issued by the Ministry of Industry, was required.

At the beginning nobody at the plant wanted to hear about my request to be transferred or sent on the business trip to Kiev. I shared my personal problem with my boss. He deeply sympathized with my heartbreak. He promised to talk with the Division Manager on my behalf, and tried to secure my transfer to the Kiev Aviation Plant.

In early January of 1946, I finally got all the required documents and was allowed to travel to Moscow. I left Novosibirsk by myself. My father, brother and sister Roza, with her family, stayed behind. On arrival to Moscow, I had an appointment with the Personnel Manager in the Ministry of Aviation Industry. I applied to be transferred to work at the Kiev Aviation Plant. His reply was that he did not have a request from the plant Personnel Department, seeking individuals with my qualification and experience.

I explained to him that I was not expecting to be hired immediately. My main concern was to reunite with the rest of my family and then to look for employment. Luck again was on my side. The Personnel Manager was very receptive to my plea. I was asked to sign a document, stating that I would not require employment by the Aviation Plant in Kiev.

At the end of January I arrived in Kiev. I temporarily settled with my brother Lazar and the rest of our relatives. My sister Tsilya and her family were about to move out. Her husband, through his employer, was promised an apartment in the building, which was under restoration. He was in charge of the project.

The first order of my business was to visit the Personnel Manager at the Aviation Plant. He confirmed that all positions, which required people with my background, were already filled by former employees who returned from evacuation earlier. I asked him to sign a release document, stating that I can look for employment elsewhere. He promptly issued the required document. Now I was free to act on my own and try to find a suitable employment.

Kiev was heavily damaged during the war. In the downtown area, all the buildings were destroyed and massive stones and bricks covered the streets. The public transportation system was not operating. The feeling was of emptiness, depression and pain.

The apartment building where Grisha lived before the war was not destroyed. I found the building custodian and asked him if he knew anything about Grisha. The only news he was able to give me was that someone else already occupied his apartment.

One day walking through the city rubble, I met Frida. She also came back to Kiev from Novosibirsk. I shared with her what was on my mind and in my heart. Frida offered to help with my search.

We went to the Address Directory Office to look for the addresses of the individuals with Grisha's last name, living in Kiev. We were given a list of addresses of the individuals with the same first and last name. Frida and I went to every address. Only disappointment awaited us.

I went to the local Military Office, and gave the officer in charge Grisha's field military address, which was in his last letter received by me. I was told that the office would conduct an inquest and let me know the results. A reply was never received.

I wrote a letter to Grisha's parents address in Donbass region[14]. Shortly, I received a reply from their neighbor. The family had not returned from the evacuation. He did not know where they are. I tried every available resource in my search for Grisha, but without success.

I began looking for a job, which would provide me with the living quotas. I was desperate to bring my father and brother back home from Siberia.

In a relatively short time I was offered a position of Deputy Manager in the industrial engineering department of the Supply Company for the textile industry. I decided to accept this position, and continued looking for a job, which would better suite my interests.

The main office of the company was located in downtown Kiev. One day when I was returning home from work, I saw a classified ad for the position of a Manager in the Industrial Engineering Department for the newly created Office of the Wood Processing Industry. After the war, I dreamed of finding employment in the business that would provide me

---

14 Donbass is coal and steel producing region in eastern Ukraine.

with new challenges. I knew there would be many obstacles to start a new career, but decided to apply anyway.

The next day I walked into the building of the Office of the Wood Processing Industry and asked for direction to the Personnel Department. I met a Personnel Manager and was given an opportunity to fill out an application for the position. He introduced me to a Chief Engineer of the company, who was temporarily functioning as a Director.

The Chief Engineer told me that he was not familiar with the responsibilities of the new position and was unable to make a decision, if I qualified for the job. He suggested that I went to the Ministry of the Wood Processing Industry. He stated that if they would approve my credentials for the position, then I should come back and we would continue our conversation.

I went to the Ministry of the Wood Processing Industry. Instead of going to the Personnel Department, I asked for an appointment with the Manager of the Industrial Engineering Department. The Manager was a big, tall man, who just recently retired from the military service.

At the beginning he did not take me seriously. He was trying to explain all the difficulties associated with the job in this position, especially for someone who never worked in this industry before. I replied that I was not afraid of the new challenges, that I was single and would spend as much time as required to learn the specifics of the new industry.

The Manager told me that he needed some time to think it over, and asked to come back the following day. During our next meeting, he informed me that at the time it was very difficult to find qualified candidates to fill the vacancy, and he would take a chance to recommend hiring me. On my job application he wrote that he was not against my candidature for the position.

When I returned to the Office of the Wood Processing Industry, the Chief Engineer was still not ready to make a decision. He decided to protect himself from the responsibility even further. He told me to go to a local branch of the Engineering Society Office for further review of my credentials.

I was disappointed, but had no other choice. During an interview I was asked about my education and previous work experience. At the conclusion, the Secretary wrote his comments on my application, stating that he was not against my candidature. I was hired for the position of Manager in the Industrial Engineering Department.

Many former experienced employees did not return from evacuation. I had three individuals working in the department. One was my deputy, a young man, who recently was discharged from the military service. He graduated from college just before the start of the war and did not have any practical experience. He was happy when I was hired. I took responsibilities for the work of the department off his shoulders.

This was a position of high accountability. More than twenty factories were under my supervision. Some of them were located in the territories, which just after the war became part of the Soviet Union. Many were in the Western Ukraine.

I made a decision to visit each factory. I wanted to meet people, look at the equipment they worked on, and gained knowledge of the products, which each factory was manufacturing. I frequently traveled to the remote and dangerous areas. Some of them still had enclaves of guerrillas fighting against the Red Army, trying to disrupt annexation of the territories by the Soviet Union.

The majority of the factories were almost completely destroyed and without an adequate number of the experienced workers. All the efforts were directed to resume furniture production, which was in high demand. After completion of the inspections, I invited Managers from these factories for meetings in Kiev. We discussed how to implement timely restoration of the facilities and to resume full scale production.

I encouraged experienced Managers and workers to assist those who were new to this industry. They provided much needed on the job training. This created an atmosphere of mutual support and friendship among employees.

I was working diligently, trying to determine the manufacturing capabilities of each facility. This resulted in the implementation of efficient production technologies at every factory, which our office oversaw. I established good working relationships with the subordinates and earned their trust and respect.

Through my employer, I was offered one room in a two-room apartment. At the time this was something to look forward to. I lived in the crowded apartment with the family of my brother. I dreamed to have my own place.

In my personal life there were many relationships. To my disappointment each of them was ending up in uncertainty. Years were passing by, and I turned thirty-four at the end of the war. All the happiness of my life was in my work, my friendships and my large family of close relatives, who provided me with their love and moral support. I was always busy and never felt lonely. I was surrounded with friendly people at work who respected me and I respected them.

Once when I was returning home from work, I met an old acquaintance of mine. I knew him before the war. He was very happy to see me. His name was Alexander. He was known by his nickname, Shura. We talked about our lives during the war and he insisted on staying in touch with me.

I told him that I was working long hours and did not have much free time. He insisted to know where I was working. One day after work, when I was leaving late in the evening, I saw Shura waiting for me outside our office building. He asked if we could meet on the weekend, and I agreed.

I also met another man through my friend Frida. His name was Victor. He just returned home after the war. He had many memories about that horrific period in his life, and liked to share war stories with his friends.

I was not strongly attracted to either of the men. My thoughts were still about Grisha and these memories were too painfully fresh. I hoped for the miracle to happen. I prayed in my heart that he was alive and one day we would be together again.

Victor looked very frail and worn out by the war. He had good manners and knew how to present himself. His intellect was more to my liking. He lived in the apartment with his elderly parents and family of his sister. He had no room of his own.

Shura was very energetic and good-looking. After several meetings together and trips to the movie theaters, each of them began to demand that I made a choice. I replied that I was not ready.

Shura asked me to marry him almost at the same time Victor proposed to me. I replied to both of them that I needed time to think everything over, and asked not to rush me. I requested each of them to stop seeing me and promised to make a decision within a month. They both agreed with my conditions. I was not in love with either man. I knew that both of them were decent individuals, but I had to choose the one closest to my heart.

I knew Shura a long time ago. His persistence and affection for me were important factors. I also knew his sister. She lost her husband during the war. She was a very lovely and hard working woman. She and her two young daughters lived in one room of the two-room apartment, which Shura was able to secure after the war.

I knew the whole history of his life. His father was killed in 1918 during a pogrom in front of his mother. Shura was only eight years old when he became an orphan. His mother, Hanna, was left with four small children. Shura was the oldest. Hanna was unable to provide for the children on her own. She was forced to place Shura and his middle brother into the orphanage. She kept the only daughter and youngest son with her.

In the orphanage Shura learned a trade. At the age of fifteen, he went to work and helped his mother to raise two younger siblings. His middle brother, who went to the orphanage with him, finished high school and went to college. His youngest brother was killed during the Great Patriotic War.

After the war, Shura became very devoted to the family of his widowed sister and his mother. He provided for them, and helped his sister to raise two young daughters. All these positive qualities of his character were highly respected by me. Physically he attracted me more than Victor. The financial side was never a concern of mine. I always was able to provide for myself.

I knew very little about Victor. He introduced me to his family. I left their apartment with very depressed feeling.

84

They lived in the basement. His father was blind, his mother was very frail, and his sister looked ailing.

During the time when I prohibited Shura and Victor to see me, each of them wrote me a letter, promising that they would do everything in their power to make me happy, and that I would never regret my choice.

I introduced both men to some members of my family. Everybody was afraid to give me advice. I knew that I had to make a choice by myself. I decided on Shura, but my heart was not filled with joy and happiness. Shura was afraid that I would change my mind and insisted that we get married as soon as possible.

We were married in August of 1947. Our daughter was born in July of 1949. I became a very devoted mother, and tried to give my daughter the best possible upbringing. I believe that I succeeded in that. As she grew up we became very close, like two best friends.

When my daughter and her husband decided to emigrate from the former Soviet Union, my husband and I joined them. We helped them with raising their children and that fulfilled our lives in the New World. My daughter and son-in-law were always very attentive to our needs, helped us with the day-to-day living and that eased our adjustment to a new life. We left the Soviet Union with the fear for our future, and found home in the USA.

Sarah with husband and daughter
1950

My mother and I during May Day Parade
Kiev, Ukraine 1959

A DAUGHTER'S EPILOGUE

My mother, Sarah Vaysberg, died on December 24, 1994. She died in the Reading hospital less then 24 hours after being admitted there. She was eighty-three years old. My husband and I visited her in the hospital two hours before she died.

Her mind was clear. She tried not to show us that she was in pain. My mother asked us to call home from the hospital. She wanted to talk to her grandson, Stan. He just came back for Christmas vacation from the Pennsylvania State University, where he was a sophomore.

My mother wanted to know if he received in the mail results of his fall finals. Despite the fact that she was very weak, she was happy to talk to her grandson and learned that the mail had just arrived and he did very well on his finals. That news cheered her up.

During our visit, my mother asked me to start looking for a nursing home, where she could be placed after her release from the hospital. She knew that I had to work and would not be able to provide care her condition required.

In a little while my mother told us that she was tired and needed a rest. She asked us to leave the hospital and come back later. My last words to my mother, before leaving her bedside were: "Mom, I love you." She replied: "I love you too. Kiss the children for me." These were the last words we exchanged.

My husband and I left the hospital with grave hearts. The thought of sending my mother to the nursing home made me disheartened.

Two hours after we returned home, the phone rang. My mother's attending physician was on line. He informed me that Mrs. Sarah Vaysberg passed away.

Though I knew how serious my mother's condition was, this news was hard to accept. I was not fully prepared for the inevitable. I felt emptiness and sadness. My loss was tremendous and grief overwhelming.

For the last fifteen years of my mother's life she lived in America. At her age she learned to read, write and speak English. She was able to pass all required examinations and became a Naturalized Citizen of the USA in the spring of 1985. She was proud to be a citizen of this great country. Her only regret was that she came to America too late in her life.

Ten months after my mother died, a local newspaper asked readers to write about what their parents did *right* in raising them, and as a child you resented, but later on in life cherished and were thankful for.

There were thoughts galore from many appreciative readers. Seven letters were selected to be printed. One of them was mine. This is what I wrote: "I was born in Kiev, capital of the former Soviet Republic of Ukraine. At the age of seven, I entered first grade of the local general education school. All subjects were taught in Russian language.

At the same time, several new schools opened in Kiev. They were called schools of foreign languages. There was one school for every major language: English, French, German and Spanish. These four schools were intended to serve a population of 1.5 million people.

The focus of these schools was to provide a general education, as well as to teach children the respective language from the first grade through the high school every day, six days a week.

Admission into these schools was difficult, if not impossible without proper connections.

My mother made the acquaintance with the Principal of the English school through her work. She and the school Principal became good friends. The Principal offered my mother to transfer me into the English school midway through the school year.

New school was far away from where we lived. School buses never existed in the former USSR. After a long walk to the tram station and a ride on the tram, I took a trolley and then walked another several blocks to school. This journey lasted about one hour.

At this school all the general education courses were taught in Ukrainian, which was different from Russian and difficult for me to understand. The English class was the most difficult. Since I entered this school midway through the third grade, I had to catch up to the kids who studied English from the first grade.

By the end of the week, with tears in my eyes, I declared to my parents that I could not take it anymore and would not go back to new school. I returned to my old school the following week.

After the end of school year, my mother called for a family council. My parents explained that by not attending the English school, I would be missing a tremendous opportunity.

The knowledge of a foreign language would culturally enrich me, expand my understanding of the different social systems and values, and ***possibly*** serve in the future as a tool of communication. A decision was made to hire English and Ukrainian tutors for summer and try new school again next year.

I started fourth grade in the English school. By the end of the school year, I was assisting other children with their English skill. I graduated from that school and went on to college, majoring in Metallurgy and Materials Science.

Seven years after graduation from college, I left Soviet Union and immigrated to the United States with my family.

Though I resented my parents' decision in my youth, I am forever grateful for their foresight and wisdom.

It is through my parents' persuasion and perseverance, that I am able to communicate freely today, using the English Language."

This letter appeared in the newspaper's "LIFESTYLE" section on December 24, 1995, exactly on the day of my mother's one year passing anniversary. This was my tribute to her memory.